CHRISTOPHER OKEMWA (ED.)

COMING OUT OF ISOLATION

POEMS ON RESILIENCE, TRIUMPH AND HOPE

VERLAG EXPEDITIONEN

Verlag Expeditionen, 2022

Christopher Okemwa (Ed.)
Coming Out of Isolation
Poems on Resilience, Triumph and Hope

Cover picture: Tobias-Tullius, Germany
Cover design Birgitta Sjöblom, Sweden
Book design Gino Leineweber, Germany

Printed in Germany
ISBN 978-3-947911-73-8

CHRISTOPHER OKEMWA (ED.)

COMING OUT OF ISOLATION

POEMS ON RESILIENCE, TRIUMPH AND HOPE

Table of Contents

Poets in alphabetical Order   Page

Preface   15

Aakash Das Sagar Chouhan (Salem, Tamil
   Nadu, India)   17
Alka Singh (Uttar Pradesh, India)   21
Amit Shankar Saha (Kolkata, West
   Bengal, India)   25
Anna Keiko ((Shanghai, China)   29
Anuradha Bhattacharyya (Chandigarh,
   India)   33
Arif Khudairi (Cairo, Egypt)   37
Art Goodtimes (Colorado, USA)   39
Ayo Ayoola-Amale (Lagos, Nigeria)   41

Basudhara Roy (Jamshedpur, Jharkhand,
   India)   45
Beata Poźniak (Beverly Hills, California,
   USA)   49
Bimal Guha (Dhaka, Bangladesh)   53
Biplab Majee (Midnapore/Kolkata, West
   Bengal, India)   57

Cao Shui (China)   63
Carol Gieg (Benicia, California, USA)   71
Chad Norman (Truro, Nova Scotia,
   Canada)   75
Channah Moshe (Jerusalem, Israel)   79

Dai Yuese (Shanghai, China)   81
Dan Brook (San Francisco, California,
    USA)   83
Daniel Brondo (Buenos Aires, Argentina)   87
Daphne Barbee-Wooten (Honolulu,
    Hawaii, USA)   91
David McVey (Milton of Campsie, East
    Dunbartonshire, Scotland, UK)   93
Debaprasanna Biswas (West Bengal,
    India)   95
Dee Allen (Oakland, California USA)   99
Dennis Nurkse (Old West Road,
    Arlington, UK)   103
Dola Bajpayee (Jharkhand, Jamshedpur,
    India)   105
Dorit Weisman (Jerusalem, Israel)   107
Dragan Dragojlovic (Belgrade, Serbia)   109
Dwi Wahyu Candra Dewi (Blora, Central
    Java, Indonesia)   113

Eileen R. Tabios (Saint Helena, California,
    USA)   115
Eliza Segiet (Tomaszów Maz, woj.
    Łódzkie, Poland)   119
Ernesto P. Santiago (Athens, Greece)   123

Gabriel Chávez Casazola (Bolivia)   125
Genny Lim (San Francisco, California,
    USA)   129
Germain Droogenbroodt (Altea Town,
    Alicante, Spain)   133
Gili Haimovich (Givattaim, Greater Tel
    Aviv Area, Israel)   137
Gino Leineweber (Hamburg, Germany)   139
Giti Tyagi (Karnal, Haryana, India)   145
Gomado Koku Hola (Lomé, Togo)   149
Grace Murray (Forfar, Angus, Scotland,
    UK)   151
Gui Qingyang (Hangzhou, Zhejiang,
    China)-   153

Hayim Abramson (Bet El, Israel)   157
Honey Novick (Toronto, Ontario,
    Canada)   159
Hussein Habasch (Afrin, Kurdistan)   165

Imali J. Abala (Westerville, Ohio, USA)   169
Ivonne Gordon Carrera Andrade (Quito,
    Ecuador)   173

Jack Ogembo (Kisii, Kenya)   177

Jane Beatrice Ovbude Ejim (Tralee
    County Kerry, Republic of Ireland)   179
Jaydeep Sarangi (Jhargram, West Bengal,
    India)   183
Jim Landwehr (Waukesha, Wisconsin,
    USA)   187
Joan McNerney (Ravena New York,
    USA)   191
John Curl (Berkeley, California, USA)   195
John Tunaley (Manchester, England, UK)   199
Joseph A. Farina (Sarnia, Ontario,
    Canada)   203
Julio Cesar Paz (Cienfuegos, Cuba)   207

Kahtan Mandwee (Rochester, Michigan,
    USA)   209
Karlo Sevilla (Quezon City, Philippines)   215
Kate Young (Chatham, Kent, UK)   219
Kathleen Herrmann (Vallejo, California,
    USA)   221
Kay Ritchie (Glasgow, Scotland, UK)   225
Ketaki Datta (Kolkata, India)   229

Laksmisree Banerjee (Ashiana Gardens,
    Jamshedpur, Jharkhand, India)   233
Lee Kuei-shien (Taipei, Taiwan)   239
Les Wicks (Mortdale, NSW, Australia)   243
Linda M. Crate (Meadville, Pennsylvania,
    USA)   245

Lorraine Garnett (Jamaica, West Indies)   249
Lucille Lang Day (Oakland, California,
    USA)   253

Marcelo Sánchez (Frankfurt am Main,
    Germany)   257
Mare Leonard (Kingston, New York,
    USA)   261
Mark Fleisher (Albuquerque, New
    Mexico, USA)   263
M Chambers (Guisborough, North East
    England, UK)   267
Miguel Ángel Olivé Iglesias (Holguín,
    Cuba)   269
Molly Joseph (Kerala, India)   273

Neelam Saxena (Pune, Maharashtra,
    India)   279
Nicola Frangione (Forenza, Italy)   283
Norbert Góra (Jastrzębia, Poland)   287

Old Captain of Three Gorges (Baotou
    City, Inner Mongolia)   289

Peggy Morrison (San Francisco,
    California, USA)   291
Peter Londi Lwal (Kisumu, Nyanza,
    Kenya)   295

Pravat Kumar Padhy (Bhubaneswar,
  Odisha, India)   299
Preety Sengupta (Ahmedabad, India /
  New York, USA)   303
Purnima Kulkarni (Pune, India)   305
Pushmaotee Subrun (City, Mauritius)   311

Ranko Pavlović (Banja Luka, Bosnian and
  Herzegovina)   315
Raúl Henao (Medellín, Colombia)   319
Ravindra Pratap Singh (Uttar Pradesh,
  India)   323
Ronny Someck (Tel Aviv, Israel)   327
Richard Marvin Tiberius (Tai) Grove
  (Brighton, Ontario, Canada)   329
Rie Sheridan Rose (Austin, Texas, USA)   333
Runa Pathak Uppal (New Delhi, India)   335

Sahaj Sabharwal (Jammu City, J&K, India)   339
Sally Quon (Kelowna, British Columbia,
  Canada)   341
Sangram Jena (Bhubaneswar, Odisha,
  India)   343
Setaluri Padmavathi (Hyderabad, India)   349

Shakes Khan (Nanjing, China) — 353
Shruti Goswami (Haldia, West Bengal, India) — 355
Sourav Sarkar (Cooch Behar, West Bengal, India) — 357
Sudeep Sen (New Delhi, India) — 361
Sue Zhu (New Zealand) — 363
Susheel Kumar Sharma (Allahabad Prayagraj, UP, India) — 365

Thryaksha Ashok Garla (Chennai, India) — 369
Tuwanda Muhammad (Atlanta, Georgia, USA) — 373
T.W. (Shangai, China) — 375
Uditi Naagar (Chennai, India) — 377

Vickie Ya-Rong Chang (Berkeley, California, USA) — 379
Virginia Fernández Collado (Almeria, Andalucía, España) — 383

Wang Fa (Tangyuan, Heilongjiang, China) — 385
Winston Farrell (Barbados) — 387
Wang Yagang (Shangai, China) — 389
Yudit Shahar (Petach Tikva, Israel) — 395

About the Editor — 399

Preface

The alarm and the horror that characterized the years 2020 and 2021 are fading fast, gone, or about to go, while the gentle footsteps of the Guardian spirit can be heard yonder. Images of spring, sunlight, blazing candles, brilliant flowers, and moonlit nights are taking center stage in our minds. There is hope for a better life, and a healthy situation in the world in 2022 as people start to gather on the streets, hugging and kissing; their mask-less faces display laughter, giggles, and beauty. In incredible abundance, life has come or is soon coming back, rushing in, bending down to pick up its old cloth.

With the availability of vaccines and the removal of isolation restrictions in many countries, the lethal claws of the virus are no longer dreadful as it has been in the last two years. This new anthology, Coming Out of Isolation: Poems on Resilience, Triumph & Hope, features poems written by poets after their endless days in lockdown and self-isolation. The poems herein express the poets' feelings and thoughts in a completely new way with a healing tonal quality, brighter and pleasant imageries, and new lively metaphors.

For two years, the world has been lying in the cold hands of death. Over three million people globally have succumbed to the virus. We have been subjected to statistics about the dead and the infected. We have been told to flatten the curve. We have been advised to keep social distance. We have been warned of dire consequences if we don't wash our hands. Each time we enter a building, we come face to face with notices such as "Wear Your Mask!" and "Sanitize Here!" Many, who die, die alone in bed, far away from home, and have no chance to utter their last words to their loved ones. It has been devastating, scary, and lost meaning in life. Although some countries have once again gone back to lockdown recently, on the whole, we can infer that corona is dead or about to die, and poets have found new ways of expressing themselves in this anthology.

Here you will witness that literature can express this new life, a new description of images of happiness, triumph, and hope. Unlike the first anthology, Musings during a Time of Pandemic: A World Anthology of Poems on Covid-19, in which poets painted a grim situation of the world, this collection is replete with images of stars, moonlight, sun, and roses. Featuring poets from five continents, Coming Out of Isolation, Poems on Resilience, Triumph & Hope give various ways poets abhor the horror phase of the pandemic. They are now celebrating the brilliance of the new life. Life can smile again.

Poets in this anthology shout precaution as we move out of isolation. They recommend that people, vaccinated or not, asymptomatic, immunocompromised, or covid-infected, keep the covid-19 precautions. As the celebration of the triumph over the pandemic starts, continues, or continues after that, poets highlight that people will still be hospitalized, in intensive care, and at once need ventilation support. The jubilation should not throw all care into the air. As we celebrate life in abundance, let's take the gentle hand of the divine angel as we grope along through this dim-lit dark phase of life.

Christopher Okemwa
Kisii University

Aakash Das Sagar Chouhan
(Salem, Tamil Nadu, India)

The poems by Aakash Das Sagar Chouhan have been featured in Efflorescence by Chennai Poetry Circle, The Virtual Reality (Sparrow Publishers), Amravati Poetic Prism, Guntur Int. Poetry Fest and many more. He's a proud member of Soul Scribers Society that curates Yercaud Poetry Festival every year.

Five corners habitat us
His window certifies a light-beam for me
Is shadow a friend of mine?

Gunshot sky holes blamed
Illuminati interrogates
Atmosphere introspects
Who're you?
Were who been we?
Who am I? Yes, yet to be.

So eyes all meet betwixt brows
Crows' isolation
Beak to beak solitary dove downloads olive twig(s)
Unmasking I.P. addresses
Lie detective inboxes
Weave stomata's
Sieve thoughts
Live and let live.

BOW & ARROW

A ray of hope needn't crack walls
Is hurray a coherent sound of victory?
Solitude befriends corners four with directions five
If isolation is monogamous monopoly
Buoyant gravity.

Aspirations aim to fail not tails this tale
My untamed tongue toddles to blame
Darkness opt Big Ben's eyes
The center is alone to spread lonely strands
Utopian lies.

Alka Singh
(Uttar Pradesh, India)

Alka Singh is an Assistant Professor of English at Dr. Ram Manohar Lohiya National Law University Lucknow. For her writings and expressions, Alka Singh has ten awards to her credit. Her works in criticism include *Postmodernism* (2008), *Gender Roles in Postmodern World* (2014), *Postmodernism: Texts and Contexts* (2014), *Issues in Canadian Literature* (2016), *Women Empowerment* (2018), *Women: Issues of Exclusion and Inclusion* (2018) and *Women Society and Culture* (2018). She has also published a poetry collection called *Colours of Blood.*

AND THE WORDS GREW STRONGER

And the words grew stronger
under the mighty spiritual spell
the urge for peace
the urge for pace.
The self to find a better space,
systems longing for breath a fresh.
The mortals again for a spiritual rush.
Nature, benign and merciful,
nature shall bless-
and it is the umpteen bliss.
The world grows stronger
under the spiritual spell.

ALTRUISM TO SAIL

Rays gleam for words
the values grew
on the fertile brethren land.
The peace to prevail
altruism to sail.
Hope has wings, and so it soars
high, higher up to the climax.
The land of peace to entail
full rainbow—the brightest and the mightiest.

The dark dull phase;
the nightmare …
soon to give a beginning new.
The words move on
and the image is seen—
a healthy tomorrow;
quite powerful and sheen.

Amit Shankar Saha
(Kolkata, West Bengal, India)

Amit Shankar Saha is a widely published, award-winning poet and short story writer in English. He has been nominated for the Pushcart Prize, the Griffin Poetry Prize, and the Best of Net Anthology. He is the Editor-in-Chief of EKL Review, the co-founder of Rhythm Divine Poets, the Assistant Secretary of Intercultural Poetry and Performance Library, the Chief Executive Editor of Virasat Art Publication, and the Fiction Editor of Ethos Literary Journal. He has a Ph.D. in English from Calcutta University and teaches in the English Department of Seacom Skills University.

FADING DARKNESS

The muezzin sounds
the marching footsteps
of the invading day.
A lonely sweeper
sweeps off the fag ends
of the smoky night.

In the old book in
my mind a new page
flickers like a star.

Will the fading darkness
once more write a script
undecipherable by light?

UNWALKED FEET

So let us go to the pub then
and celebrate this sin
of seeing you again.
But will you have time for a swig?
There's something frazzled feisty in
what we drown down our throats
in the cocktail of drinks
which spikes our blood as well as whims.
Will you keep time locked in your palms
and not allow the old
days hold the balustrade
and walk across the balcony?
This illicitness that absconds
from the attics of minds
and loiters on these streets
still remembers the unwalked feet.

Anna Keiko
(China)

Anna Keiko studied law at the School of Political Science and Law, Shanghai East China University. She is a Member of the Shanghai Pudong Writers Association, Founder and Chief Editor of Shanghai Huifeng Literature Association, Chinese representative and director of the international cultural foundation ITHACA, the Chinese representative of Immagine & Poesia in Italy, Member of the Board of Directors of the Young Writers Magazine, and Member of the Board of Directors of New Literature Alliance. Her poetry has been published in over 30 languages in approximately 190 newspapers and magazines. For her poetry, she gained international awards.

SUNRISE OF HOPE

Translated by Germain Droogenbroodt

The light of dawn
erases the traces of the night
relentlessly, time goes on flowing
although I wish it would stop
like a picture fixed by the camera's lens
because as valuable like fruit in a tree is life
Like the moon ascending at night
so you are, my love, whatever happens
wherever you are, I keep you in my heart
since I am in love with you my world has changed
because two hearts found a home of tenderness
sunrays play on the heartstrings of love
lighting up the dawn of hope.

A DROP OF WATER

February 14, 2021
Translated by Germain Droogenbroodt

A drop of water
Dripping day after day
The creek became the sea

A ray of light
Shines year after year
A small seedling becomes a big tree

An encounter
A white sheet alike meets a colored pen
Drawing a spring full of love.

A BEAUTIFUL SAKURA

The most ingenious of painters
Painted last night a marvellous painting
Even the poor stop and admire
April's beauty, nature's masterpiece
A creature of heaven,
An angel descended on earth.

Anuradha Bhattacharyya
(Chandigarh, India)

Anuradha Bhattacharyya is a widely published Indian writer. Twice awarded by Chandigarh Sahitya Akademi for her novels One Word and Still She Cried, she has authored five books of poetry, four novels, two academic books, and several short stories. She has also been awarded Chandigarh's State Award, Sahitya Shree, and Poiesis Award for Excellence in Literature. She is an Associate Professor of English, Postgraduate Government College, Sector-11, Chandigarh, India.

GIVE ME A ROSE

I shall give you a surprise
One day, my love…

When the sky is not downcast
And the fields aren't swaying in fright,

When my search for the best
Prize in the world is over
And the way ahead is clear,
I shall have a glimpse of the finest
And the purest of affections,
When the long-sought treasure
Of the jealous dragon is retrieved
And the fiercest beast in man
Is slashed to death,
I shall find the heart in me
To collect my dues
And claim my latitudes,
When all is painted in bright hues
And my returns are pleasurable,
Then, my dear, then I shall,
And never forget me until then,
I shall present you the perfect surprise.

What if the blue sky never appears
And the fields fear the incessant storm?
What if the prize of the day is won
By another
And the foggy days trouble us,
Where shapeless and imperfect nature pursues,
While the beast safeguards the dragon's snare?
Would you scale the toughest peaks
And be granted your dues,

Figuring what makes a perfect picture
Exactly?
Then, failing all the promises, then
What will surprise you?
What will you do?

When the grey sky groans
And the rough ways torment
I shall carry on with the only thing
That gives peace
And perseverance
And I shall take the brush in my own hands
To challenge the color of ruin,
Restoring the loss of a dream
With perfect love.

Then,
Not forgetting me for a single moment,
Strengthening your heart
With my love's strength,
Capturing your dreams,
You travel as distant as you wish,
While I wait holding the perfect treasure
Right here,
With a gift more nearer
More comforting than any other,
A token of the purest affection
One could gather;
I ask you now
Not to wait for another day
But celebrate the present hour
And give me a rose.

Arif Khudairi
(Cairo, Egypt)

Egyptian poet, novelist, short story writer, playwright, literary critic, fabulist, editor, and translator, Arif Karkhi Abu Khudairi (better known as Arif Khudairi) is a professor of Arabic literature; with more than sixty-two books to his credit, including five Folk Tale collections and nine poetry books in Arabic. Arif has participated in international poetry festivals in Asia, Africa, Europe, and Latin America. His works have been translated into twenty languages. Arif Khudairi is an accomplished translator.

WE WILL PREVAIL

In spite of all that
Which defies us,
Here and there,
In spite of
The darkness,
The suffering,
And the pain,
We will prevail,
For we believe
That after darkness
There will always
Be light,
After hardship
There will always
Be an ease,
And we believe that
Whatever befalls us
Now and then,
We will prevail.

Art Goodtimes
(Colorado, USA)

Poet, weekly op-ed columnist and former Green Party elected official in Colorado, Art Goodtimes served as San Miguel County Commissioner (1996-2016) and Western Slope Poet Laureate (2011-13). Former poetry editor for Earth First! Journal, Wild Earth and the Mountain Gazette, currently he's poetry editor for Fungi magazine and co-editor with Lito Tejada-Flores at the on-line poetry anthology SageGreenJournal.org. Retired from political life, Art serves as trustee and program director for the Telluride Institute.

COVID WINTER SOLSTICE

Got to see it big eye-lensed
at Danny's Fruita observatory
Hay bales eight feet high smeared
with mud & shaped, rounding one around
& into a central viewing courtyard
to block out surface photon static

The rings of Saturn & moons of
Jupiter side by side in the Great Conjunction
The heavens coming together
Even as we go on pulling ourselves
apart
The gravity of our discontents
stronger than all our shared histories
Yes we will wobble, Capt. Barefoot agrees
We will blur, but let's hope we work ourselves out
This experiment we call a species, a template
adapting as we are to Earth's every niche & peak

May we too
resume a reciprocal place
in the Chthulucene pantheon
even as our immediate cosmos appears
about to be spinning back into Anthropocene orbit
as galactic information arm of the heaven's Milky Way
Shaking hands. Hugging, Like planets
in the Goldilocks Zone
of the stars we are

Ayo Ayoola-Amale
(Lagos, Nigeria)

Ayo Ayoola-Amale is acknowledged as a poet for positive social change. She enjoys going into schools as a committed advocate of poetry who has seen the critical role that poetry plays as an important catalyst for learning, stimulating creativity and in developing vital communities. Ayo's poems have appeared in several international anthologies, journals and magazines and have been translated into many international anguages. Her poems are concerned with confronting the problem of violence, racism and the breakdown of human community.

IDLE LAKE

It's just how I do it
in my mind, out of what I have molded into,
   like an idle lake
what has moulded into me starving my brain of
   blood
in the wide river of life.
It's just how I do it
locked in windows, doors, gates, jammed
like I went through a great flood
I let myself in even with my heart jumping out
   of my chest.
dragging along my tangled legs and dress suit in
   a virtual film show.
Then again, with stories of what yesterday used
   to be.
Am I more formed into a kind of life on a
   playing ground for ghosts?
deserted like an abandoned bridge,
my quiet self, embrace,
only I can do so to unlearn living like a cheetah
   in a zoo.
Am I an addict, or a fool mutating?
Stuck between the desert and the mountain,
   a door broke open,
my legs wobbled like a drunkard.
 My perseverance need be praised
Won't be too proud though—
aloneness is a shadow.
Only I can lift every voice souled within
   and true
until heaven and earth tremble
I'll sing hallelujah like Leonard Cohen,
until liberty rise higher than the skies,

with a freewill loud as a yawning thunder.
My spirit endured the pain of cutting the feet
from the limbs once i dare to walk out of
    the gate,
that kept me like *Hammurabi sculpture* museum,
    of tired years,
with the corner of my jaws flowing with quiet
    tears,
then reshaped how i swallow balls of pounded
    yam, in thinking, and mind
My body now brings me into light and new
    mornings,
drowning the blurred night of my soul.
To let myself out like the wind, free.

Basudhara Roy
(Jamshedpur, Jharkhand, India)

Basudhara Roy is an Assistant Professor of English at Karim City College, Jamshedpur, Jharkhand, India. Her areas of academic interest are diaspora writing, cultural and gender studies, and postmodern criticism. She is the author of two collection of poems, *Moon in My Teacup* (Writer's Workshop, 2019) and *Stitching a Home* (Red River, 2021).

THE SUN, THE FIRST GLORIOUS SUN OF 2021

Tai, your picture shows you
reclined on a snow covered
picnic table, drinking in the
sun, soaking it up like a
sponge while the sun, in turn,
seems to be drinking in Kim,
a warm *chai* on a chilly day.

That tree in the background,
covered in a fresh blanket of
bright snow, is lapping up the
sun too even as it hugs its
whiteness tight like a proud
brass-buttoned coat.

I have never seen snow but once
in Yumthang, the Valley of
Flowers at our country's hilly
fringe. I was twenty-five and
tendrilled with the yearning to
know snow, I realized I wasn't
exactly prepared for that wonder
of white stretching around me
like love's seamless dream.
When I tried to shut my eyes,
the white had seeped into them
too so even my dark was now
dressed in a drape of light. Funny
what that snow can do to you!

Your pictures, however, send me
more snow than I have ever seen
before! It is there, a lazy cloud,
sprawling over everything as it
looks for a place to snooze,
filling every corner it finds,
every curve, every fold, and
here, continents away, my skin
grows cold anticipating its need
for heat. But you, it seems, are
good friends with it. You let it
lie about as it pleases, while here
in my sun-drenched home in
Jharkhand, I am always putting
winter away into a box and
stuffing it in the attic to be
opened every ten years or so.

SUN-BOUND

To thee, wayfarer of light,
that chase the brilliance
of a thousand suns,
darkness is but a rare hour
in the relentless succession of days
as success-studded, glory-borne,
you claim the hopeful wealth of brightness.
If perchance, however, ominous clouds
should choose to gather upon your ways;
if promises should be dimmed, and
the dancing rays shred to dust;
do not then hesitate, to call on me
for I haven't changed my address.

An inhabitant still of these
faithful plains of darknesses,
my refuge shall be yours.
And together once more, we shall read
those unlearned hieroglyphs of waiting,
till your hope strikes roots
and your sun, rises again.

Beata Poźniak
(Beverly Hills, California, USA)

Awards and received five Voice Arts Award nom for narrating Penguin Random House and Scholastic's audiobooks. She writes and directs experimental film poems for which she was acknowledged in the recent encyclopedic book: *The Poetics of Poetry Film*. She holds a Master of Fine Arts Degree and served on the faculty at UCLA and USC in Los Angeles, USA. She is a human rights activist and introduced the first bill in the history of US Congress to recognize officially International Women's Day in the United States. Beata Poźniak is a performance artist, activist and poet. She won two Earphones.

RADICAL GRATITUDE

What you want—Wants you

A city strangled by cars, highways and smog
A city cushioned by memories of lockdowns, BLM crowds and
  lost jobs
People are hurt and want to be heard

A city sweeps memories
Under the beds of poked hearts
And its layers of remembrances
Deep down, deep down. Deep down.
Down. Down deep.

A city with humanity frozen to its marrow
Moving deadly homeless thoughts
That crawl out of their bedless shelter
Experiencing joy of the pulsating earth
Once again.

Breaking out of the mold
The discordant sound of the riotous birds
Fly around
Facing the sky, seeking hope.
Face down
Begging for a cosmic hug.
Spiritual fitness blossoming with power and beauty
Receiving kindness is one of the most challenging things to
  accept.
What moves people the most is
Kindness.

Radical forgiveness and gratitude

After all, we are all a gift of nature.

TO GO BEYOND THE MASK ITSELF

A two-way traffic mask
Contact with a face
that is not your face

A mask that
affects me
A mask that
affects you
A mask? Although motionless
is breathing life
Sends a message
in and projects
a message out
A meeting
of a reflection
of an echo
that becomes
a distorted mirror
A mask that
affects the wearer
A mask that
affects the observer
Masks fed by centuries
of tradition and wisdom
Spiritual journey.
Sacred imagination.
Ancient feelings.
A quest for gratitude
immersed in the sacred
well of the soul

Bimal Guha
(Dhaka, Bangladesh)

Bimal Guha is one of the leading poets of Bangladesh. Without following the regular paths of his predecessors, he creates his own way and style. After the liberation war of Bangladesh, he was one of those who helped transform Bangladesh's poetry into a newer consciousness.
Bimal Guha was born on 27 October 1952 in Bangladesh. He has a Ph.D. in modern Bengali poetry from the University of Dhaka and has 33 books published, including 13 poetry books. Bimal has received several prizes and honors for his literary contributions.

OH, WORLD GET UNITED TODAY

Third World War has begun!
This war is neither the worldwide violent outcries of a vehement
bear
This war is neither the bombing of trillion-dollar nuclear
warheads,
The opponent of this war is invisible microscopic killer virus
The frenetic dancing Corona worldwide!
Do Aliens from the unknown planet spreading terror to us?
Will our lovely planet forcibly be taken away by others?
If this pandemic is the outcome of a wrong research instead
If rumors are proven true someday
Then humans have to pay for the disaster plethora.

The whole world is dire frightened.
Why do people build lethal weapons obnoxiously
At the climax achievements of civilization?
Why do people stock deadly nuclear weapons?
This question is for the civilized world
This question is for the welfare of states!
The majesty of science is oppressed by nuclear powers
How easily superpowers accept the motion of destructions
No rules are negotiable to those miscreants
Even diplomacy has been defeated to the evil power!

Still have time
If the human come back to the nature
That would be a great achievement.
The arms races should come to an end from today.
This war is the people's war against the deadly Corona!
If humane races need to fight for existence
Against the revenge of the nature
Oh, world you get United today.

OH CORONA

Oh corona, take me if you want to
I'm writing down all your awful deeds.
Suddenly, I know not how, you spread
Plumes of smokes blackened the world
What is the bravery you have?
Moved through the clandestine path
You entered into a different empire
Unexpectedly, before any comprehension
And spread-out poisonous fume
Ignited flames of wrath, in diverse directions
Corona, I spit on your face

Remember
Human beings can never be defeated to death
They know how to embrace death easily
Valiant never bow heads and clasp their hands
They are engaged in defensive battle
Today I write down the detail descriptions
For the next generation.
Someday those who will read your dreadful deeds
I shall spit to your face with sheer indignation.
Your route will be clogged easily
Shall take over the duties of the Earth with intellect
Then your entry to the Earth will forever be forbidden.

Biplab Majee
(Midnapore/Kolkata, West Bengal, India)

Biplab Majee was born on 30 May 1947 in Tamluk town. He got a degree of Bachelor of Science from the University of Calcutta in 1971 and a Teachers' Training Diploma in the Russian Language from Moscow State University, USSR in 1976-1977. Biplab Majee is a poet, prose writer, and lit. critic and translator. So far, he has 28 poetry books, 36 prose books, 16 translated books, six children's books published, and edited eight books. He received eight International, one Indian, and nine local awards and honors.

DEATH IS NOT THE LAST WORD

Translated from Bengali to English
by Nandita Bhattacharya

Death is not the last word.
Life has some hope and aspirations
Life also has some memories of dream
Blowing away death
Life becomes a turbulent sea sometimes.
The earth will get back
the memory, dream and future.
Men will be liberated from the life of animal.
Look out. There is an emerald blue sky.
Birds are Twittering there.
Butterflies, grasshoppers and crickets are there in the garden.
Getting rid of mask, sanitizer
men are again coming back to the seas, hills, forests, picnics
    parks and the festivals of shopping mall.

Life is becoming new normal again.
Resurrection takes place repeatedly in life.

Death is not the last word …

LEAVING BEHIND
THE FESTIVAL OF DEATH

Translated from Bengali to English
by Nandita Bhattacharya

Leaving behind the festival of death
The new days and the festival of life are coming back.
The green EMU trains those are lost at the blue horizon in the
  new year
returning at the Midnapore station again.
Leaving behind the loneliness of the year of covid-19
Those desolate rail stations are again full of noise.

Leaving behind one year of lock down of Corona virus
which is but a bad dream.
People sans masks come back to the market, shopping mall,
the invisible pairs of birds show up at cinema halls, theaters and
  entertaining parks once again.
You have also come out spreading the wings like a butterfly.
Men once again stand with their heads high as well as with
  majesty
under the blue sky
stretching as far as the horizon,
The aircrafts are flying in the sky
The ships are there on the banks of the Seven Seas and Thirteen
  Rivers.
Good bye to the Covid year which appeared with the loneliness
  of thousand years
and putting on the mask of death.

We will resurrect with the vaccine of love…

THE MONUMENT OF OYSTER

Translated from Bengali to English
by Nandita Bhattacharya

I saw you first amidst the
       blue twilight for the first time
You were flying towards the ocean
       spreading your blue wings
I thought at my first sight
       that there was either a nymph
or a mermaid
But no, you were a woman
who was travelling from my own town
towards a town at the seaside

Though you appeared like
       a young seagull to me
Since then, thousand years have
       passed away
I stand alone
like a symbol of a fossil of
an oyster monument…

MY LOVE RESURRECTS
WITH THE ADVENT OF WINTER

Translated from Bengali to English
by Nandita Bhattacharya

My love resurrects with the advent of Winter.
Sitting in Midnapore I discuss with
Ernest Hemingway about the Marlin fish
caught in the fishing rod.
The very Marlin fish brought
the Noble prize for him.

The love can be resurrected at any country of the world during
   winter
When I mate with you in the sunlight
Numerous events like in a novel started taking place.

Moving round and round the Sun the love which was born
   during winter forwarded the odor of the civilization of
   Harappan in every house of Midnapore.

The feelings like fire jumped to my body from yours…

Cao Shui
(China)

Cao Shui, also Shawn Cao (born on June 5, 1982), is a Chinese poet, novelist, screenwriter, and translator. He is a representative figure of Contemporary Chinese Literature. So far, 20 books of Cao Shui have been published, including five poem collections, three essay collections, ten novels, three translations, and one hundred episodes of TV series and films. He is also chief editor of Great Poetry, deputy editor in chief of World Poetry, secretary general of Boao International Poetry Festival, and vice president of the Silk Road International Poetry Festival. He lives in Beijing and works as a professional writer and screenwriter.

THE CRY OF BATS:
THE FALSE CROWN IS SWINGING

Beijing, January 20, 2020
Musing on the
Epidemic Situation of Novel Coronavirus

I was humming and dancing in the pool
Trilobites swayed gently 500 million years ago
Gilgamesh was swinging with his axe
The Roman Augustus swayed in his crown
The Chinese emperor swayed with the jade seal
This is what I saw with my eyes closed
Soft trilobites
The backbone rises in the middle
The ribs spread out on both sides
Cambrian animal explosion
Jurassic dinosaur extinction
The bat spread its wings and glided
We are moving in two spirals
The soul lands on the earth
Looking for the right body
Enki and Ninmah combine in Summer
Adam and Eve are married in the garden of Eden
Isis and Osiris make love in Egypt
Naga and Nagi of India embrace each other
Isis and Serapis of Greece are interdependent
Fuxi and Nvwa in China get married
Two spirals of gene droop
Pairing of adenine and thymine
Guanine and cytosine are linked
DNA and RNA rotation
I fell asleep in a daze
The dragon head with long beard told me:
Don't worry about Mesopotamia
Don't worry about Persia, India and China

Don't worry about Judea, Egypt and Greece
Don't worry about Bodhgaya and Jerusalem
Don't worry about Moses, Jesus, Confucius, Shakyamuni,
Muhammad
The bat suddenly spread its wings and howled in the dark
The novel coronavirus appears in a false crown
There is a cause, there is a result
Where there is a friend, there is an enemy
I was you, you are me
Who woke up in today's water
Like a trilobite swaying in the sea
The bat spread its wings and glided

THE HEART GROWS BLUE ZHUGE FLOWER

March 29, 2020 in Beijing

We were imprisoned in a castle
Only I was allowed to go for a walk
I walk on the bright grass
See the wild flowers all over the ground
The blue flower is like a silk scarf
The green leaves are like feather fans
They say it's a smart Zhuge flower
Named after the wise Zhuge Liang
I picked a bunch of Zhuge flowers
Sneak into our castle
It's on your head
You will be queen
You will have wisdom
As long as your faith is strong enough
The heart grows blue flowers
We are wearing blue Zhuge flowers
Dancing in the lonely castle
The whole sky revolves around us
The whole universe is gathering above us
There's nothing in the world we can't do

GOD'S LAND IS BECOMING WASTELAND

Written in Beijing on May 4, 2020

I walk in God's Land
China is in a depression
I roam in the streets of hometown
Shops on the street closed
I stand in the spring
I feel the cold wind blowing
I stand in the capital
I feel desolate
I walk in the crowd
Feel lonely forever
I walk on the street
I feel empty
I want to cry
But no tears
God's Land are overgrown with weeds
The land of my country is desolate
I sighed in a low voice
God's Land is Becoming Wasteland
God's Land is Becoming Wasteland

THE FORBIDDEN REPUBLIC OF THE WORLD

February 27, 2020, Beijing

We live in the Forbidden City
No entry here
We look at Tiananmen Square from Tiananmen tower
People are dancing Great Dance of Sorrow

You stand center stage
They all push you towards sorrow
Backstage, some play the accompaniment
Behind you, some dance to the funeral music
Standing center stage crying, there's only you

This stage stands center of the Asian continent
You are on the Pamirs Plateau wailing
People come from all directions
Asians play funeral marches for you
And Europeans dance along
Wishing for death, you stand there

You are the most ordinary person
Yet no one will let you be
They sing for you, dance for you
To aid your sorrow process
Until you give up all hope
Until you depart this world
They'll grieve briefly and leave
To find the next eulogy

I suddenly woke up from a thousand and one dreams
See the prisoner in the cell Dance: Great Dance of Sorrow
I continued to sleep
You live in the Vatican
No entry here
You look at St. Peter's Square from St. Peter's Church
I saw them singing in Italian through the iron windows:
La danza dell'immenso dolore

They live in Great Mosque of Mecca
No entry here
They looked at the Worshiping Courtyard from the Kaaba
  House
I can see from the iron window of Chinese characters
I saw them singing in Arabic through the iron windows:

رقصةُ الحُزنِ العظيمة
I wake up repeatedly in my sleep
Language unfolds like a flower in Wikipedia
I hear the Babylonians sing: ت
(Arabic)رقصةُ الحُزنِ العظيمة

The Jews are singing:
ריקוד עצוב גדול (Hebrew)

The Persians are singing:
رقص ناراحتي (Persian)

The Egyptians are singing:
kederin Ulu dans I (Turkish)

The Indians are singing:
दुःख का बड़ा नाच (Hindi)

The Greeks are singing:
Μεγάλος Χορός της θλίψης (Greek)

The Chinese are singing:
大悲舞 (Chinese)

Roma is singing:
La danza dell'immenso dolore (Italian)

Chang'an is singing:
La Grande Danse de la Douleur (French)

Byzantine is singing:
Magnus saltus animae (Latin)

Beijing is singing:
> Gran Danza de la Tristeza (Spanish)

Vienna is singing:
> Großer Tanz der Trauer (German)

Seoul is singing:
> 대비무 (Korean)

Moscow is singing:
> печальный танец (Russian)

Kyoto is singing:
> 悲しみのダンス (Japanese)

We live in the People's Republic of the World
People are imprisoned on the earth
We become the Forbidden Republic of the World

Carol Gieg
(Benicia, California, USA)

The topic of traumatic brain injury has been inundating the media lately. Carol Gieg is an author and a poet, whose memoir is written from an insider's point-of-view. She suffered a traumatic injury to her brain, had neurosurgery, survived and is thriving. Carol's book, *TBI-To Be Injured-Surviving and Thriving After a Brain Injury*, inspires and educates those who have sustained such an injury. She includes research about the genesis of new neurons and pathways within the brain and tips on how to encourage these processes to happen. She currently lives in Benicia, California with her husband, Luis.

HOPE ON THE HORIZON

I consider the state of the world as I walk on the beach each
morning;
Seeking respite from the worries endlessly plaguing my troubled
mind.

Lost in thought about tomorrow and tomorrow, my solitary
steps traipse,
On an endless shoreline washed in waves of despair.
A heavy jacket shields me from the frigid air, though it is
springtime.
Profligate actions of humankind are the culprits of climate
change.

Hegemony pits country against country as millions of people
suffer,
The tyranny of despots, yearning for power and smothering
compassion.
Science is denied by our leadership and his sycophants,
Threatening our very existence on this fragile planet.

The days pass and, finally, there are other footprints in the sand,
Loneliness surrendering step by step, as we support others in
their anguish.
The sturdy ship of recovery plows through the turbid waters of
COVID-19.
We are destined to reach that hope on the horizon,
Crossing the finish line, humanity is the victor on the other side.

DESPAIRING, BUT NOT WITHOUT HOPE

September, 2020

There is a war being battled today, against a foe so formidable,
So agonizing, sometimes fatal, this smallest and most prolific
    form of life on Earth.
How can we disaffiliate ourselves from a threat so resistant to
    cure,
As it deracinates the very roots of who we are as unique?
We have no defense against its insidious action,
A parasite unable to live without using the mechanisms which
    define us,
Forcing our cells to reproduce it, as we are sorely tempted to
    capitulate hope.

But, in spite of these devils, their deprivation inspired,
The human race continues, our pleasure still sought and attained.
Ours is the choice to hold tight to our dreams and hopes for the
    future,
For ourselves, for our children, for the planet and Life.
Look around, we see people not surrendering, not forsaking
    what they love,
We are still making bucket lists; poetry festivals abound.
People of faith stage "Zoom" meetings to retain communal
    spirit,
We travel, not on planes to overseas adventure, but enrich our
    lives at National Parks closer to home.
Lovers still love; friends and family support those whose losses
    are great.
Vicarious hugs and social media eradicate loneliness many a
    time.
So, rough as the road, there are still rescuing side streets,
We carry on, in altered form as is our choice,
Discovering value in each and every moment,
Choosing not only to exist, but to live.

Chad Norman
(Truro, Nova Scotia, Canada)

Chad Norman lives beside the high-tides of the Bay of Fundy, Truro, Nova Scotia.

He has given talks and readings in Denmark, Sweden, Wales, Ireland, Scotland, America, and across Canada. His poems appear in publications around the world and have been translated to Danish, Albanian, Romanian, Turkish, Italian, Spanish, Chinese, and Polish. His collections are Selected & New Poems (Mosaic Press), and Squall: Poems In The Voice Of Mary Shelley, is out from Guernica Editions.

BIRDER IN THE CATHEDRAL

How am I a part of this?
Any other lost one
could be at the path,
but snow holds us back.

Sadness is a ball inside,
no dancing, or any boy
trying to master the shot.

A weight I feel
and it hurts on days
when clarity kisses the poet.

Inside where both live
so far from the chase
for any money to pay
the bills, to worry over.

A glance up works
it is there in the trees
or on the wires, it is
the relief and escape.

And when the sun is out
it agrees, the crow families
tell of want, tell of how to
be part of a sunny hour
other than what enslaves,
to see how few clouds
can free the sky
above our painted.

IF DANDELIONS ARE WEEDS

1.
The ability to touch one's finger
comes with the day I asked
without stopping a girl with blue shorts
if dandelions are weeds?
Some would hope her answer
was yes, but not mine—
if you pay attention to the sky
you will find your questions
all answered.

2.
To convince the crows
I don't want to step on
anything now trying to grow
and calling for the chipmunk
has left me only a mystery:
did he/she only come
because it was a cold day
or am I left to decide
what may have been a visit
was because my fingers
held a peanut knowing reasons
we met in the first place,
or voices hunger has
only for those in the Wild
I cannot hear or understand
even though they're loud
for those I cannot stop
in the snow or sun
looking for, hoping to honor;
it is sadness I sit with,

no visit, no further education,
convinced Spring is with my longings.

3.
One last long haul of my potion
I always bring to learn
new ferns entertain, and robins
sing relentlessly to the sun.
A day lands with little wind
and I go about the visits
all of the forest allows me,
to what's left of its green stage
or perhaps being painted above
on the sky's gift, being no more
or less the ceiling of a cathedral
I chose to sit and stay still under.

4.
What to do with faces driving by
unable to chase other than
what their politicians promise
signing cheques when possible
as the virus continues to ask us
to shoot chemicals in our arms
and believe our lives are freed then.

Far off, what the weather-guy said
is now settling brightly behind
what my daring eyes easily detect,
a few watchful crows ride the wire
no different from other florid days;
if dandelions are weeds
I continue to disagree, a beaming man
beside new blooms, healing and yellow.

Channah Moshe
(Jerusalem, Israel)

Channah Moshe was born in Jerusalem, Israel. At the age of twenty-two, she left for The American University in Washington DC, where she accomplished a B.A. in Psychology, a Certificate for Teaching English as a Second Language, and a Master's degree in Fine Arts. She spent her formative years in London and La-Tour-de-Peilz. Currently, she resides and works in Jerusalem as an editor and translator. She considers herself fortunate to have had poems published in the USA, UK, India, Italy, and on the Internet. Short stories and interviews she conducted and wrote appeared in the "In Jerusalem" section of *The Jerusalem Post*.

COMING OUT
VICTORIOUS INFECTIOUSLY DELIGHTED

Come, hold my hand
and let's go hear the band
Enjoy the crowds around
as sounds of merriment abound

Masks all tidy in the storeroom
while plans to frolic boom
Travel to the countryside
without rules by which to abide

Schoolchildren in the playground
have once again their pals found
as they chase each other
without zooms with which to bother

Exotic Thailand, Vietnam
and so many others beckon
we spread our wings
and let adventures begin

Delicate and precarious life
can be endangered by strife
only visible under the microscope
now a matter of the past, we hope
as with freedom, health and tomorrow we elope.

Dai Yuese
(Shangai, China)

Dai Yuese, a native of Shanghai, assocciate professor; member of China Modern Literature Research Association and member of Shanghai Writers Association. He has won numerous awards including Poetry Silver Award of the "Shanghai May 1st Cultural Award". He has published two collections of personal poetry entitled "Shanghai, Please Listen to Me" and "Urban Cuckoo"; and has also found his way into the collected works of "Fifteen Poets in Pudong".

BEING GOOD

Translated by Gui Qingyang

One
Only by a door or a road, undoubtedly
Am I separated from good or virtue
Thus keeping indoors myself in isolation
Or bearing along the way the noise horrible
Until one day at the funeral of one contemporary
With the eulogy so beautiful, I take on anxiety:
Being obsessed all my life with beauty
I seem to know nothing about it
Two
When the worshipped good or virtue
Is suddenly pronounced as evil
While in a blink a certain evil
Suddenly turns out to be an admired virtue
I have to swear to heaven
We must trust in nothing but time
Never believe in oneself
Never believe in MLM

Dan Brook
(San Francisco, California, USA)

Dan Brook, PhD teaches in the Department of Sociology and Interdisciplinary Social Sciences at San Jose State University in California, from where he organizes the Hands on Thailand program. His most recent book of poetry is *Sweet Nothings*.

ZIESEN RAT BROOK

A sweet little being
entered our home
enlarged our family
melted our hearts
increased our love
A sweet little being
brought us great pleasure
for one brief season
Even now gone
she'll always be with us
Ziesen Rat Brook
is a sweet blessing

HERO?

An infusion of love
accompanied by the sting of hate
soothing, burning, pacifying, piercing
sweet and sour, singing and smiling
pain and pleasure inextricably linked
mixing inside of me
mixing my insides out

a cacophonous cocktail
of comfort, confusion, & cruelty
sweating, panting, silently ranting
feeling the anxiety, expecting magic
floating and flying above myself
parts of me are laughing
parts dying

the rock that I can rely on
is the rock that cracks my skull
heroine is my hero—
yet also my nemesis
what seems to save me
insidiously invades me
I need an infusion of love

Daniel Brondo
(Buenos Aires, Argentina)

Daniel Brondo was born in the city of Buenos Aires on 1st of May 1954. He is married and has two children and a grandson. He started writing stories in1985 and showcasing his works at literary workshops and competitions. After several years later he started writing poetry. Since 1998 until now he has been participating in literary contests. He has won prizes and has been offered publication of his works in Argentina, Chile, Peru, Venezuela, Brazil, Spain, and the United States.

THE TRENCH

Long, dark roads.
(Some parts with sun)
Tours also in the rain.
It is our unequal path of struggle …
Outside the little enemy
that grows in our body
if it invades us.
Is it tiny light that I see?
Perhaps.
But we must continue towards it.
How long? Only God will know.
We are sad and disarmed.
Our weapons are coming
like vaccines …
While we are holding the road
as we can.
We see the doors as we pass …
They appear on our sides.
The red doors of pain
the green doors of hope,
the gray doors of boredom,
the black gates of death …
Our shoes dodge the pits
made by jerks
who seek, unconscious or not, your evil.
And there are many … to our grief.
We have been walking for almost a year
keeping us from the virus and from them …
But we will go out …
That tiny light will grow gigantic
and the sun, that of every day
will be for us the winners,
rewarded with life itself.

THE ACROSTIC OF NEW TIME

Unforgettably will be these moments without hope.
Today is a glorious day because we are live, in the road
Out of danger of death in our body and soul.
Painful memories not remain over our heads
Increase the feelings of resurrection
and now we demand happiness for all!

Daphne Barbee-Wooten
(Honolulu, Hawaii, USA)

Writer, Attorney and Activist lives, writes, practices and publishes in Honolulu Hawaii, near the slopes of Punchbowl. She is married and loves to dance, travel and write. Her roots include African (DNA says Ghana), Chikasaw and Choctaw (Native Americans First Nation people), British and Scottish ancestry.

COVID 19 WARNINGS

"Stay Inside"
"Wear Masks"
"Wash Hands"
"No Hugs'
Looking outside my bubble
I see
Sun shining, , grass growing , flowers blooming, colors, clouds,
rain and rainbows.
I feel the wind, hear birds chirping, nature sounds
I am so tired of watching humans
on the computer screen,
Talking to a computer zoom meeting
does not compare to a warm hug or a hello kiss.
Friends die
While I hide.
It is hard to stay
In my cave
Waiting for tomorrow
To live.

David McVey
(Milton of Campsie, East Dunbartonshire, Scotland, UK)

David McVey lectures at New College Lanarkshire in Scotland. He has published over 120 short stories and a great deal of non-fiction that focuses on history and the outdoors. He enjoys hillwalking (i. e. hiking), visiting historic sites, reading, watching telly (i. e. TV), and supporting his home-town football (i. e. soccer) team, Kirkintilloch Rob Roy FC.

WHITE SAILS

We volley east along the M8,
part-sprung from lockdown.
Beached around the airport
are shoals of white bodies
with shark tailfins, liveried
in British Airways red and blue.
They wait for the pandemic's end,
for the return of lost travelers.

The Braehead car parks sweep past
and the chessboard hospital tower
looms ahead. Something is wrong.
White and long and tall, are these
sprawling new-build flats? Thrown
up hurriedly, planning regulations
ignored, like ranting street orators?

No, not 'buildings', but cruise liners
laid up in the old King George V Dock.
They angle southwest to catch the dying light.
White sails in the sunset, they await the
all-clear. When will their clients find the
courage to mount the gangways again?

They may linger there for a while yet …

Debaprasanna Biswas
(West Bengal, India)

Debaprasanna Biswas is a Bengali poet, born on January 24, 1948 in Katwa, India. He was brought up at a Raina a rural environment that must have influenced his acquisition of a human nature and impacted upon his style of writing. When he was a student, he edited a literary publication, Banasabha (meaning, "meeting within the forest"), during time which he met many renowned poetic legends of Bengal. In 2019 Biswas won 'Best Writer of the Year' award, given by Bangabhumi Sahitya Parishad, an esteemed literary group, Dhaka (BD). Biswas is also an active member of Central committee, International Council of Human and Fundamental Rights (ICHFR) in India.

HOPE AND TRIUMPH: NEW EARTH

I like to translate your thirst
The thirst for education
Thirst for livelihood
Thirst for upliftment
Thirst for quarries to overcome
After corona pandemic world-wide
We have changed our system of education
Have discovered ourselves not to be suppressed.
e-learning already substituted class teaching
Pollution comes down as gathering is controlled
Political leaders depended on virtual meeting
New system of marketing has been improvised
Rushing to big city gets its alternative
Rural survivability is getting oxygen
Mask culture has grown removing dust pollution.
Self-realization has now been honored.

BLUE STAR

I am in search of a blue star
Only one blue star in the Milky way
Milky way my eternal path of life
The endless path of destination.

I am in search of a blue star
One and only one among the stars
That will radiate secret blue flame
With constructive criticism without blame.

I am in search of a blue flame
Flame that conquers NextGen world.
A blue star from destitute of road side
That will give a lesson on existence.

I am in search of a blue star
That will come forward with a voice of silence
Uphold their basic needs
Create a wider horizon.

I am in search of a blue flame
Flame within the poorest
With academic brilliance
In the mankind of ego less religions.

I am in search of a blue flame
Which will illuminate at night
So smugglers feel embarrassed
Threatened to give up their practice.

I am in search of a blue star
Most probably the pole star
Which will be the compass
In an ocean with stormy night.

Dee Allen
(Oakland, California USA)

Dee Allen is an African-Italian performance poet based in Oakland, California. Active on the creative writing & Spoken Word tips since the early 1990s Dee Allen is an author of five books and 26 anthology appearances under his figurative belt so far.

EMERGE AGAIN

W: Hiroshima Anniversary 2021

We've become a nation of sore shoulders
With Band-Aids™ from all
Our cost-free
Dates with the nurse's needle,
Our key to salvation
From the early grave.
Gloved hands.
Alcohol swab.
Sterilized spot
On bare skin.
Inject deep.
Injection
So we can
Enjoy life again,
So we can
Feel sun's warmth
On our faces,

So we can
Leave the domestic
Cages of homes,
So we can
Feel the breeze
In a good run,
So we can
Revel in Summer
And its greening process,
So we can
Visit again
All parts of nature,
Including the half with
Gates shut to us for months,

100

So we can
Filter into
Clubs, museums, theatres, libraries
Opening their doors to us,
So we can
Relegate the words
"Lockdown" to distant memory,
"Quarantine" to be forgotten,
So we can
Bring ourselves
To a state approaching
Safe, good health to attain,
So we can
Keep ourselves
From hospitals
And morgues,
So we can
Deny the underground
Worms of premature feasts,
So we can
Come together
Without fear of infection,
Take injection
So we can
Act the part
Of the human family
All days of the year,
So we can
Emerge again
From hibernation
We never wanted.

We have
Emerged again
Recovered.

American life
In real-time
Rediscovered.

But don't shout too soon.

Delta's roaming, ferocious,
Right around the corner.

Be prepared. Stay safe.

Dennis Nurkse
(Old West Road, Arlington, VT, UK)

Dennis Nurkse is the author of eleven poetry collections. His poems have appeared in The Times Literary Supplement (UK), The New Yorker, Poetry Ireland, The Paris Review, The American Poetry Review, Poetry London, and other journals. He has received fellowships from the National Endowment for the Arts (USA) and was a finalist for the Forward Prize (UK). He has also worked in human rights, and was the author of At Special Risk: The Effects of Political Violence on Children in Haiti, commissioned by the Lutheran Immigration and Refugee Services.

CONVERSATION BEHIND THE WHITE CURTAIN

I will protect myself and my family.

I will bury ninety gallons of fresh water,
stash rice and beans in steel boxes,
hide a bike with freshly oiled gears
to glide between the rows of stuck cars

says one voice:

I will keep a gun with a single bullet

says a second voice:

I foresaw this all my life but when it came
I could not recognize it—it had the face
of wind and rain, the shining face of days.

I want to go back to who I was,
the house with a beehive in the pines,
the brook breaking all night over stones.

Let me go back to the child swinging,
the dog digging, the cat hiding under the car,
the cloud of moths—take me back! Accept me.

The ants help each other—they carry fat crumbs,
bury their dead and sweep their narrow paths.
The wasps can recognize each other's faces,
you and you, in the chaos of the swarm.
The bees dance a language: here is nectar.

I want to go back to being a body. A voice with eyes.
So we say. But we all speak at once.

Dola Bajpayee
(Jharkhand, Jamshedpur, India)

Dola Bajpayee is a writer, editor, publisher & singer. He is the founder and Director of 'Sur O Sahitya' (cultural events, literary meets). He has been honored by Nikhil Bharat Bongo Sahitya Sammelan, jharkhand Ranchi Bangla Academy, Bangla Academy, Kolkata, Rabindrasadan, Nandan Shishir Manch & Vishwabharati Shantiniketan, Rabindrabharati Kolkata. He has been invited to attend many literary meetings, International Book Fair Dhaka, Kolkata International Poet Organizaton PEN. He has written the following books: *Kalpamanjuri* and *Juktanjali*.

RAINBOW

Belligerent world, belligerent minds
I lost my poem,
I lost my song,
I lost my existence
In a dark room blind brain
With the dreadful situation
Lost my life, bonds, and dancing eyes
Lost tingling sensation
Lost chirping and waving sea
Still we live we rise

Mortal poison, the blue voice,
Billowy repetition, restoration
Dhanavantari (mythical physician)
Holy vessels and human life

We find inspiration in the words
Whisper, laugh rejoice with you…
The 'Rainbow' heart throb, when
Dances in to sky in exotic-colored Costumes; Our mind twist
and whirl
To the throbbing music of colors.

Dorit Weisman
(Jerusalem, Israel)

Dorit Weisman lives in Jerusalem, Israel. She is an award-winning poet, a multidimensional writer, a novelist, a translator, an editor, a filmmaker, and a literary organizer. She has published ten volumes of poetry, two prose books, and two translated books and received international literary awards. She is the editor of three social poetry Anthologies. Her poems have been translated into English, Italian, French, Spanish, Turkish, Arabic, Albanian and Georgian. Since 2013 she has been the founder and editor of the Poetry Program on Israeli TV (Channel 98), which runs several weekly times.

AFTER TWO CATHETERIZATIONS

From the book *Scrambled Eggs in Jerusalem*
Cohel Publishing house, 2017

Translation from Hebrew to English: Joanna Chen

Shabbat morning, the street is silent
I stroke your back

Lingering over the valleys between your shoulder blades
We do not mince our words in the act of love
And we have our own ways

But now your heart is different.
It has five metal stents
Along two coronary arteries

The ivy leaves outside redden

I listen to your every breath
Anxious you do not exert yourself

I want you for many more years
Smooth and muscular and beneficent as you are now
As you always were
Following me through the desert for forty years.

Later, by the kitchen sink, naked
Together peeling potatoes for the oven—
The grandchildren will soon be here.

Dragan Dragojlovic
(Belgrade, Serbia)

Dragan Dragojlović was born in Serbia. He graduated and obtained Master's degree in Economics from Belgrade University. Dragojlovic translates poetry from the English language and lives in Belgrade. He has published 23 poetry books in the Serbian language, five novels, three books of short stories and a few children's books. His poetry books have been published internationally (in USA, China, India, Italy, Poland, Greece, Turkey, German, Swiss, etc).
He receives many literary awards in his own country and four from abroad. He is a member of the Serbian PEN. He became member of Academy of American Poets, 2008.

JOY SOARS INTO THE SKY

Am I sleeping or is it just a delusion?
In my room—my quarantine cell
I am constantly listening out for the
Corona viruses invading from everywhere,
knocking on doors and windows,
secretly weaving a wreath of sham flowers,
strewing the streets with deadly roses.

Instead of panicking, I plead for
patience, patience, patience ...
Cooperation and solidarity between countries,
among people, cooperation and solidarity,
love and compassion!
This will shrink the spreading of the virus.
And despite being an insidious killer,
It cannot be immortal, either.
As I soliloquize so, playing safe,
I fasten masks on windows,
on my face, on my heart,
as do people around the world.

COVID'S LEEWAY DWINDLES.

Suddenly I hear laughter and voices,
people walk the streets freely,
carrying syringes and vaccines.
Covid 19 viruses shriek and scream.
The isolation doors reopen.
The world seems to have changed.
I join the singing neighbors.
Joy soars into the sky.

VICTORY OF LIFE

Isolation of the world from itself
lasted forever and a day.
For long, some defied the deadly corona,
claiming it was all fictional.
As though no one wanted to know
what was happening,
the world seemed to lack
attentiveness and patience
to recognize
the invisible executor of the death warrant,
devoid of self-control
and responsibility,
as though we needed time
to perceive that the sick and dead
were constantly rising in numbers,
many did not realize that
the virus forgives neither folly nor ignorance.
It fiddled about with us until, at one point,
the sum of human knowledge appeared
packed in small vaccine vials
and blocked its way
to depriving humanity of its path,
a path on which the struggle of life and death
has not yet been won, nor is it time-limited,
the path we must take
with discipline and vaccines,
with faith and perseverance
to finally banish from earth
the relentless messenger of death
and begin writing poems about happiness,
and not about the Corona virus,
writing poems about life,
and not about isolation and death.

Dwi Wahyu Candra Dewi
(Blora, Central Java, Indonesia)

Dwi Wahyu Candra Dewi, born in Blora, Central Java, Indonesia, May 8, 1983. Creating poetry for him was an opportunity to express the truth through literature. Meaning and taste united in words to make life more colorful. The writer is a lecturer at Lambung Mangkurat University Banjarmasin, Indonesia. His works have been published in the anthology of poetry with poets locally, nationally, and internationally.

FREEDOM MISSED

Indonesia, December 15 , 2020

No more cheerful children in the field in front of the school
No more soul-touching advice on them
No more bells to sign for school entry and return
There are no more sports or ceremonies for common health
Lonely and quiet, the school is just a magnificent uninhabited
    building
The longing for the teacher was unstoppable
Students are no longer guided
Will there be another occupation?
Corona freezes the world
Corona destroys plans
People lost their jobs
Children cry milk can't be bought
Officials feast on corruption
Gone is conscience
Cries of tears are commonplace to release a loved one to heaven
Bloods and wounds scratched on the holy heart to always let go
    of what happened
Freedom from sickness becomes hope
The freedom to greet the world from knowledge and insight is
    always awaited

Eileen R. Tabios
(Saint Helena, California, United States)

Eileen R. Tabios has released over 60 collections of poetry, fiction, essays, and experimental biographies from publishers in 11 countries and cyberspace. She has also been translated into 11 languages and has edited, co-edited, or conceptualized 15 anthologies of poetry, fiction, and essays. Her writing and editing works have received recognition through awards, grants, and residencies.

EVERYDAY NEW YEAR'S RESOLUTION

The end of a year
should raise our chins
for more blows

for we are not
in the business of dying
until we are dying

… and a kiss
might lose its way
to land on us

COVID'S FIREFIGHTER

my story is in
water, as bones
Waters by William Allegrezza

My story is not in
fire, as bones
from gutted trees

as the sooty sketch
of a fallen bird's wing
splayed atop a rock slab

as the new stone ruins
rising from the felled
once ivy-covered winery

as a memory doomed
to battling itself
to survive—

Thus, this poem is for water
shape-shifting to flesh
out what stubbornly remains:

a concrete wine barrel
its makers long-dead
but still tall, belying
the ashes that surrounds

Eliza Segiet
(Tomaszów Maz, woj. Łódzkie, Poland)

Eliza Segiet graduated with a Master's Degree in Philosophy and completed postgraduate studies in Cultural Knowledge, Philosophy, Arts, and Literature at Jagiellonian University. The author's collections, *Questions and Sea of Mists,* won the title of the International Publication of the Year 2017 and 2018 in Spillwords Press. Eliza has been nominated for the Pushcart Prize 2019 and the iWoman Global Awards.

NEW OPENING

Translated by Artur Komoter

She stopped planning,
waiting and dreaming.
Her monotonous time
it became overwhelming.

In the evenings she whispered:
      – No future anymore.
      Time to die?

Everything apart from her?

It is not too late yet
to do something,
to get to know a fraction
of the world's secrets.

Every day is
a new opening
—not a time to shut the longings
in unaccomplishment.

In the beginning she chose Georgia.
Delighted with the beauty of
Tbilisi, Batumi, Poti
—she breathed more fully.

She already knew that
the wind of her strength
will become the
previously unattainable goals.

TURQUOISE

Translated by Artur Komoter

Our eyes
need sight.

Body–feelings.

Mind—
a treat from everyday life.

Work–home, home–work.

Someday one must say:

enough.

Where has joy hidden?
Between the sense and nonsense of life?

A long-lost paradise
needs to be revealed.

So far and at the same time so close
time can be measured
with the high and low tides
of turquoise.

To live, live
to at least

restore the meaning.

Ernesto P. Santiago
(Athens, Greece)

Ernesto P. Santiago spends all his free time here and there trying to learn something. He is too small for his ego. He is enough for himself. His verse has been widely published and anthologized in print and online. He lives in Greece, where he continues exploring his senses' poetic myth.

OUT, OUT OF ISOLATION

Endless controversies over masks,
pandemic surging through the mind,
but know in darkness I must bask
and not cower in fear as if resigned.

My love, life and I may not have
much freedom and energy as of today,
but I make not a reason to misbehave
because there's always a good way.

While recovering from isolation
isn't quick or easy look of the eyes,
yet I have control and affirmation
with my happiness than I realize.

I try to find myself, more lessons
to myself; again hopeful and formal,
for now is a battle of all weapons
between old and new normal.

Born with elements of nature,
I, from womb that cares for all alike like art,
greet all species alike with pure
smile without regret of heart.

Oh, I see where I can be as I am
as I know of myself what I am best—
for I am beautiful when I am in blossom,
when I am at peace I am at rest.

Gabriel Chávez Casazola
(Bolivia, 1972)

Gabriel Chávez Casazola (Bolivia, 1972) poet, essayist, cultural manager and journalist, is considered "one of the essential voices of contemporary Bolivian and Latin American poetry". His books were published in 14 countries and his poems have been translated into 10 languages as well as the Braille language. He is curator of the International "City of the Rings" Poetry Meeting of the Santa Cruz International Book Fair; professor of the Creative Writing program of the University of Santa Cruz (UPSA) and directs the poetry workshop "Llamarada verde".

KOYU ABE PLANTS A SUNFLOWER SEED IN THE
JOENJI TEMPLE GARDENS

Translation from Spanish by Katherine Hedeen

Koyu Abe, in his hard black tunic,
shaved head held high
straight brow
plants a sunflower seed in the Joenji Temple gardens.

He calmly places the small shell filled
with potential light
with future wonder
in a tiny hole dug in the ground.

Covers it with a small shovel
waters it with an orange watering can.

A breeze blows over the Joenji Temple gardens
Koyu Abe feels it on his water-splashed hands.

In a cloth sac at his thigh he carries
some tens or hundreds of seeds.

It's still early in the morning and his task is to plant each one
and to cover each one
and to water each one with his orange watering can.

Soon a million sunflowers will carpet the Joenji gardens and the
neighboring plots.

Monks, field workers,
everyone is sure to have hands dampened by the water irrigating
the children's
future yellow wonder,

hands that will be compassionate lights for exhausted eyes.

Koyu Abe doesn't know Van Gogh, but he paints sunflowers
with his shovel.
Koyu Abe, whose eyes make out the gray profiles of nuclear
silos in the distance.

At the edges of Fukushima the Joenji Temple gardens rise
and it's urgent to purify the sky, purify the waters, purify the
ground, purify the suns planting sunflowers.

It isn't for looks Koyu Abe tells me in the silence of this image:
The roots absorb the heavy metals
and from the poison a flower is born.

But it is also true that beauty purifies
by itself

quotes the Dutchman, emerging from the silence of the canvas,
and Koyu Abe hands me a bag of seeds
shells filled with tiny light.

Van Gogh hands me
the giant orange watering can.

Genny Lim
(San Francisco, California, USA)

Genny Lim is San Francisco Jazz Poet Laureate emeritus. Her most recent poetry-music collaboration, *Don't Shoot! A Requiem in Black,* dedicated to Black Lives Matter premiered at SF Jazz Center in April 2018 with musicians Marshall Trammell, Francis Wong, and rapper, Equipto. Lim is the author of five poetry collections, and the play, *Paper Angels,* which aired on PBS television in 1985 and has been produced throughout the US, Canada and China.

STILL HERE

Ten thousand soldiers
circle the Capitol perimeter
in preparation for Civil War
a raging pandemic and
glacier melt turned jellyfish soft
What will happen to this generation?
We are fish in the jaws of a shark
trembling in a feeding frenzy
of threatened extinction
Each afternoon I come to the pier
2000 miles away from pixelated Images
of flash mobs storming streets
Corporate greed from bad to worse
Ahead of me, the open Pacific
I do my qigong and observe the
harbor seals leaping and frolicking
in the blue sanctity of water
Their sleek, black torsos arcing mid-air
Diving In and out of the shimmering
Blue scrim of the sea
Their barks muffled by growl and pound
of bulldozers and jackhammers colonizing
land and air behind the eroding jetty
Electric scooters and bikes
whizz down the path of the pier
Joggers race past, look straight ahead
unaware of distant bobbing heads
appearing and vanishing out of the
corners of their eyes like apparitions
conjured from the indigo scarf of the sea
Suddenly, up pops in front of me
a luminous, mahogany head
with curious eyes fixed on me

Breathing in, my heart races
breathing out, behind my mask
Gently, I move with the swaying surf
She plunges back into its depths
and all trace of her disappears inside
a plume of rippled silence
I feel her presence, feral, primordial
A shadow pulling me deep into myself
And it is why I call her she
Still here, the sea, the seal and me
Captives on a vanishing canvas
One moment in time
In the divine machinery
of natural order
Unframed by pixels
Undefined by borders
Water has no boundaries
Her untamed kingdom is wild
with creatures that inhabit her
that leap in naked exultation
in looping somersaults of pure joy
Without doubt or hesitation
Without malice or ambition
above and below and across
the wide expanse of sea
complete and absolute in
this communion of
beautiful life with
all that breathe

Germain Droogenbroodt
(Altea Town, Alicante, Spain)

Germain Droogenbroodt is a Belgian poet living in Spain, translator, and promoter of international poetry. He received many international awards and is yearly invited to the most prestigious international poetry festivals, recommended in 2017 for the Nobel Prize of Literature. He has written 16 books of poetry published so far in 20 countries. The Indian poet-publisher Thachom Poyil Rajeevan compared his philosophical poetry with the poetry of Rabindranath Tagore, whereas in Spain, his poetry has been compared with Juan Ramón Jimenez. According to Chinese critics, his poetry is TAO and ZEN.

CERTAIN UNCERTAINTY

Sometimes it seems
as if spring doesn't want to come

that it is wintry
or autumnal

but spring will come
if it is not erased

in us.

DON'T COUNT ME AMONG THE ALMONDS

Make me bitter,
count me with the almonds
The Unrest of the Word
Paul Celan

Don't count me among them,
don't count me
with what was bitter
or too dark.
Don't count me among the bitter almonds.
Give me,
when the night is too dark,
the light of the stars
and the hope of dawn,
the poppy of the dream.

Gili Haimovich
(Givattaim, Greater Tel Aviv Area, Israel)

Gili Haimovich is a bilingual Israeli poet and translator with a Canadian background. She is the author of nine poetry books, three in English and six in Hebrew, and a multilingual book of her poem, Note. Her poems are translated into more than 30 languages, and published worldwide in anthologies, festivals, and journals. She won the international Italian poetry competitions, a grant for excellency by the Ministry of Culture of Israel (2015), among other prizes and grants.

SURPRISING RELIEF

Translated from Hebrew
by Dara Barnat with the author

I want to speak of him love,
but how can love be words.
Love like ours is a touch.
But in the touch of words clashing on the computer screen
there isn't the same surprising relief.
In the undesired, unreleased tears inside me,
when he clears me,
I can breathe deeply, with room, a luxury,
in love, with surprising relief.
Our love is a surprising relief,
a sort of upgrade in the quality of life.

Gino Leineweber
(Hamburg, Germany)

Gino Leineweber is working as a poet, writer, and translator since 1998. In between, he was editor of the magazine *Buddhistische Monatsblätter* (BM) for six years. From 2013 to 2020, he served as president of the Three Seas Writers' and Translators' Council (TSWTC), based in Rhodes, Greece, and is currently a board member of the PEN Center German-Speaking Authors Abroad (formerly German Exile P.E.N). He writes in both German and American English. Since 2016, he has translated prose and poetry from English. His poetry has won numerous international awards.

LOCKDOWN SURVIVING POEM

I was walking
Around the house
And was thinking
Thinking about…
What?

I do not know

In the process
When you think,
You would not think
What you think

Later, when you think
The thing is
You think
What you thought

It's just like this:

Thoughts don't come
And introduce themselves
You have to figure it out
Figure out…
What?

FUNERAL

Make sure I will be buried
On a day like this

When the sun
Needs time
To arrive

Weary almost
From arising

But eager
To dry
The tears of the night

Ardent to embrace
The happy day

Kisses
With glossy lips
The colored leaves

Those
The wind will cause
The genes to fly

Make sure I will be buried
On a day like this

OUT OF ISOLATION

The first warm days
Millions and millions of cicadas*
Emerge from out of the soil
Where they have lived for 17 years
Now it's time for them
To climb the trees

When they are high enough
To find a suitable branch
The females make themselves
Comfortable to enjoy the spectacular view
While the males are
Still clinging to the tree trunk
Trying desperately to catch their breath

Like this one male cicada
That has stopped
For this female
That was sitting above him on a branch
And was looking around

He, instead of relaxing
After the exhausting climb,
Starts singing his brains out
Just to impress her
For a date with debauchery

The female, after a while,
Got a little bored

* Every 17 years, Brood X cicada emerge from the ground. The insects then
shed their exoskeletons on trees. They are endemic in areas throughout the
eastern United States, mainly in Virginia and Washington, DC.

142

Thought:
what the fuck—let's do it
give the singer his prize

Alas, he was **supposed** to die
after he'd got what he wanted,
She can't be blamed,
although little did she know it.
It's just a boy thing

LOST AND LOST

Her
world alone enchants her.
She doesn't notice anything happening around her.
Just enjoys herself.

But
I
am directly under her spell.

Suddenly
She
looks at me with her captivating eyes
that blossom like two flowers
in eternal serenity.

For a while
I
cannot breathe.

Her
look causes no reflection on her part.
She isn't even aware of where she is
at this moment
let alone a little consideration as to who the hell
it might be that surrounds her world:
Me

But
I
have lost myself in her forever.

Giti Tyagi
(Karnal, Haryana, India)

Giti Tyagi (b. 1976, Karnal, India) is an Editor, Creative Artist, International Author & Poetess, Book Reviewer & Translator from India. She has Masters in English, Masters in Education, M. Phil, holds a UGC-NET certificate, is a former Senior Lecturer from MM University, Ambala, India and an Educational Consultant at Karnal, India.

WHERE THERE IS A WILL THERE IS A WAY

"Where There Is A Will There Is A Way"
is a poem depicting the courage, the faith,
the surrender to the Divine that help him
to overcome all obstacles and impediments
in life and bloom like the flower which,
despite being stuck in between the hard rocks,
shows undeterred strength and faith and outcome.

Untiring efforts to spread around,
When struck a sap with hardships abound…
No sun, no soil, no air, no light,
The struggling roots with space so tight,
It yet did give a final fight,
And bloomed there a flower ever so bright!

The Faith, unfailing, that was shown,
Wasn't for nothing that lay deep instilled sown,
The hand wanting the flower halts at bay,
For the Divine reflects in each of its ray!

If not for Faith, nor the Surrender,
The bloom wouldn't survive the slightest thunder,
For all odds, all obstacles, the bloom's the brightest,
The Divine Will prevails, the strongest the mightiest!

Let no hurdle never leave us at dismay,
Let not our dreams the stumbles shall slay,
Let the Faith, the Surrender brighten up our way,
Where there is a will there is a way!

DEFEATING ADVERSE FORCES

"Defeating Adverse Forces"
is a poem depicting the value of virtues
such as calmness, equanimity, repose
and an undeterred faith in the Divine
while confronting hostility in life.

Whilst dealing with the forces adverse,
Stay calm, peaceful to the best of the capacity;
Allow not anything to disturb your poise,
Hold yourself firm, with confidence abound;
Call down peace, deep inner quietness,
Equanimity, the basis of all spiritual power is!

Inevitable are the attacks of the forces adverse,
Strengthening the determination, aspiration clear;
Resembling the tests meeting on the way,
Tread thy path with courage, faith;
Give not a reason for them to exist,
Respond not to their whims, let them retire!

Let not the hostility stop nor hamper,
The spiritual progress on the path Divine;
Confidence undeterred in the Divine help,
Aspiration is sincere, the succor defeats;
Steering you through, sure secure
A quiet call, a faith unshaken!

Gomado Koku Hola
(Lomé, Togo)

Gomado Koku Hola is a Togolese who studied American Literature at the English department of University of Lomé in Togo. He was born in 1991 at Kpètè-Zogbé, a village in the Plateau region of Wawa district in Togo. He currently teaches English at a private school in Lomé.

AFTER THE STORM

There has been a storm,
A worldwide vicious storm,
That damaged and paralyzed the forest.

It started from the Celestial Empire,
Spread worldwide with brazing fire,
And uprooted virtuous trees in the forest.

But at last, at last calm comes;
At last we can sing new hymns,
No more dirge nor elegy rhythms.

Let's burry the unvoiced fears,
Let's change the atmospheres,
For at last, at last calm comes.

Let's rejoice and praise the Creator,
He, who helped us win the war,
And afford us a blissful Empire.

Grace Murray
(Forfar, Angus, Scotland, UK)

Grace Murray was a teacher during her working life and lived in the great city of Glasgow, but has now retired to the Scottish Highlands. Here there is tranquility to write poetry, garden and enjoy nature among the glens and mountains. Other hobbies are reading, Tai Chi and wild swimming. She and her husband recently celebrated their diamond wedding.

POST PANDEMIC

We're coming out the other side,
If you read this, you have survived.
This ghastly lock-downs almost done—
Time to come out and have some fun.

I wonder if you feel, like me,
It's changed your personality?
Meetings and lectures, films and plays,
Hobbies and sports filled up my days.

Now there's a quieter, calmer me
With less to do and more to see.
I take delight in simple things—
A flower that blooms, a bird that sings.

Family and friends are extra dear.
It's such a joy to have them near.
And no more flights abroad, thank you—
The misty glens of home will do.

So yes—I've changed for good or ill.
I've learned that Nature rules us still.
The planet's bounty's ours to share
But we should live our lives with care.

Gui Qingyang
(Hangzhou, Zhejiang, China)

Gui Qingyang, Ph.D. in translation, poet, professor of English at Zhejiang International Studies University, Hangzhou, China, MA supervisor. Member of the Foreign Literature Committee of the Writers Association of Zhejiang Province; Vice President of Translators Association of Zhejiang; President of Hangzhou Translation Association; Member and FIT ID Card holder of Fédération Internationale des Traducteurs; Secretary General of Hong Kong International Association of Creativity; Vice President of the Educational Council, Hong Kong Quaity and Talent Migrants Association, member of International Academy for Intercultural Research. Author of approximately 300 research papers and a dozen of books including his Chinese rendition of Wuthering Heights by Emily Brontë.

POET'S MESSAGE

With great piety I look upwards
Paying special tribute to Homer, Shakespeare, Tagore and Li Po
With great piety I look upwards
Paying special tribute to "Homeric Epics", the classic epics in
    the world
To "The Book of Songs", the earliest collection of poems in
    China
I have read different genres, mostly with the same sentiments
The history of civilization is nothing but memory
And poetry is indeed our memory's sharp weapon

A new anti-epidemic epic commenced early in the year of 2020
Triggered by COVID-19 flowing out of Pandora's Box
Poets interpret with poems the metaphor of COVID-19 as
    flowers of evil
Poets observe with their souls the syncretism of Eastern and
    Western civilizations
Poetry has somehow become a totem of centripetal force of
    humankind
The angels in white are poets as well as warriors
The poets dashing between sunshine and darkness are also true
    fighters
Together they compose a most magnificent epic ever in human
    history
Parents are the path taken as we come to this world
The angels in white the light that illuminates our path
The poets show us the far distant shore in our life

Poetry knows no boundaries, world poets creating for the same
    earth
Poetry knows no boundaries, world poets praying for the same
    New Year

SONG OF AUTUMN

Among the four seasons,
I have a special liking for autumn.
In composing autumn poems,
I never miss the autumn sense in *Walden*.
On a certain autumn day,
Henry Thoreau left his "drop of God".

Walking into the autumn, I shake off several red leaves of
    poems,
Tasting Chiu Shui Poetry Quarterly, chewing gains and losses of
    life.
Who said no chrysanthemum, no autumn? No crabs, no
    autumn?
Where there is a golden fruit, there is autumn;
Where there is life reincarnation, there is autumn.

Oh, heart fall is the fall in one's heart,
There is heart fall even without fall
—When the polar bear will soon become a legend.
Both downstream and upstream are parts of the autumn,
Both happiness and bitterness are elements of the autumn.

Spring makes me moved, autumn makes me re-moved,
I cannot copy the poem complex of our parents,
But I can breathe the four seasons they have digested.
I am now crawling on the treasury of poetry,
With only osmanthus fragrance surging vibrantly inside me.

Hayim Abramson
(Bet El, Israel)

Hayim Abramson taught languages and Jewish studies. His book Shirat HaNeshamah (in Hebrew) and poems and stories in Hebrew and Spanish are released on the site hayimabramson.com. He published in Amaravati: Poetic Prism, Arc, Prosopisia, The Deronda Review, The Seventh Quarry, Voices, and in e-magazines and anthologies such as Contemporary World Haiku. He was a judge for the Poetry Contest of the Miriam Felicia Lindberg Memorial Foundation. He defines himself as an optimist.

8173 BROKEN LOVE AND ROSES

I gave her orchids, and she threw them on the floor
it was as in a satire, all a laughing matter
what was left for me to do?
Nothing matters when reality does not fit a dream.

I pined to find her twin,
just like her, but one who would love me.
I was lucky that it did not happen in any event
because eventually, another appeared who was more special
  to me.

When the sky falls
with broken love, the earth swallows us to despair.
Yet life is like an iceberg; much is hidden
with hope to be saved after the sinking of the boat.

As in Japan, the reality is not always clear-cut
we can even assume our loss gracefully
pick up the pieces of shattered dreams
and melt the metal with our tears to rebuild the vase.

We faint under what happened, feel fatigued
when a whole world has given us a cup of hemlock.
Nonetheless, our very thirst is quenched
if we determine to make the best orphans with a smile.

Life is strange; we do not know where to find our unique path
Our way through twisted alleys leading to an exotic garden
There we take stock to reflect
and lift our spirit admiring the roses in full bloom.

Honey Novick
(Toronto, Ontario, Canada)

Honey Novick is a singer/songwriter/voice teacher/poet living in Toronto, Canada.

Her writing has been translated into Spanish, Japanese, Urdu and French. She has been published in numerous anthologies and has ten chapbooks and eight CDs.

She is the 2020 recipient of the Mentor Award (CSARN) Canadian Senior Artists Resource Network, 4-time awardee of the Dr. Reva Gerstein Legacy Fund, and recipient of the 2020 and 2022 Community Hero Award. She is a resource artist for the Friendly Spike Theatre Band and teaches Voice Yoga.

A CAMP CALLED THE SUBLIME

"A camp called the sublime"
is a line from Liz Howard's
poem Psychogeometry in her book
Infinite Citizen of the Shaking Tent

From the profound depths of isolation
I turn the door knob leading out
to the unoccupied hallway of the unknown

My destination is to the sublime land of the
roosting swan

The hallway carpet patterns are like dizzying waves
to traverse these I need the cool confidence of
a deep-sea surfer championing the high waves
onto the exit door leading down
stony concrete stairs to the garage
where my expectant car awaits

Extending the side mirror, opening the door
I drop my bag and mold my body
into the driver's seat contours and away we go

Yes, there is a gingko tree enroute on this, our home
on native land. It is beautiful and health-giving
like many immigrants -
all living near pine, cedar, tamarack and maple
Diversity is the new buzzword

Onwards we go, me and my trusty red chariot
southbound to the shore

My apartment, my camp of the sublime womb is
warm, comforting and devoid of humans -

the tv informs me, the phone connects me
the computer beckons me to interact -
nothing replaces human contact

Once I had a dream of singing with the Exquisite Prince Mood
of the Disordered Clan
I no longer seek this fantasy
it disturbs my sense of myself
now I seek omens from the invisible "shoten zenjin"—
(the universal protective forces)—
no traffic accidents, no arguments
nothing lost
that is the message I bank on

Crossing grids of pedestrian traffic, car traffic, bikes and strollers
onwards to the highway where once stood
Sunnyside Amusement Park
I have never forgotten the merry-go-round
jumping on a moving circle was exhilarating

Finally, I arrive the camp of the sublime roost of swans
who waits for me to appear, I believe

gulls always circle over waters still or roiling
sometimes geese and ducks stake claim to their territory
but if I'm lucky, it is the swans, those other immigrants
the ones whose neck form heart to heart love stories
that bring to life the magical, mystical serenity
with a message that says
"be serene, learn resilience, show yourself in beauty
and swim, paddle,
forever value the camp of the sublime"

WINTER ALWAYS TURNS TO SPRING

162

born in a blizzard and tropical by nature
I am a child of the earth
covered in snow, ice and sleet
I endure the weight of my frozen dress
it is seasonal and will change, melt

this is my hope - change
 as long as I endure, have patience
winter will become spring
colorful, energetic, expectant

the greys, whites, stark blackness of winter
come with warnings of danger
yet, deep down the roots of all life
are merely dormant
asleep

winter, sometimes is like heartbreak
searingly cold, bitingly bitter
just enough to teach a broken heart
that when there once was love,
warmth, dreams still exist
reformatting

sometimes the eye cannot see
the life force of growth
entrusted to a darkened bare tree limb
latent, powerful yet invisible

it will once again bud and blossom
thus the promise
winter never fails to turn into spring
she always turns to spring

Hussein Habasch
(Afrin, Kurdistan)

Hussein Habasch is a poet from Afrin, Kurdistan. He currently lives in Bonn, Germany. His poems have been translated into different languages, and he has his poetry published in many international anthologies. He participated in many international festivals of poetry, including in Colombia, Nicaragua, France, Puerto Rico, Mexico, Germany, Romania, Lithuania, Morocco, Ecuador, El Salvador, Kosovo, Macedonia, Costa Rica, Slovenia, China, Taiwan, and New York City.

DA NANY…DA NANY

"Da Nany... Da Nany"
is a lullaby that Kurdish mothers
sing by their child's cradle;
it speaks of warmth, sorrow, and compassion.

Translated by Muna Zinati

My eyes were staring at the far horizon,
Choosing a star or two for you.
The angels from above knew that you are coming, blessed
With God's light, calm like his secluded corners.
They were patting my shoulder
With compassion and confidence,
And saying to me: a little patience, a little composure…
Hewa will arrive soon, wreathed with lights.

So, you came, my daughter.
You came to rob the sun its golden tiara tomorrow,
To ignite a lantern from its lashes for our future days.
You came to be the home poem, and the painting
For our quiet life.
You came to smooth out with your impish iron
The wrinkles of the heart's sheet.
You came to close the distance between me and me.
You came.
You are welcome, welcome.

Tomorrow,
I will draw your smile with an eye's brush.
I will guard you with the vigilante soul's lilies.
I will crown you an angel in the mirror.
I will spray you with perfume,
And with quince water, I will wash your feet!

Daughter,
I will buy you a small journal, and you will scribe in it
The buds of your heart and the iris of your dreams,
And I will record in it the stuttering of your words.
I will stay up by you, rocking you with warmth
And tenderness.
I will sing you lullabies.
Da nany
Da nany
Da nany
Until you fall asleep.

My child,
My little one,
My love,
I will put you on my shoulders and teach you
The language of trees!
I will listen to you.
I will listen to your early query
And your small letters that look like a bird's mouth.
I will take care of you as I take care of the flowers of love.
I will plant you in the word's vessels
And cover you with the petals of poems.

My daughter,
My child,
My little one,
My friend, welcome!
Welcome,
Welcome in the eye, the soul and the heartbeats.
Welcome…

Imali J. Abala
(Westerville, Ohio, USA)

Imali J. Abala is a writer and Professor of English at Ohio Dominican University (ODU) in Columbus, Ohio. She currently serves as Editor-in-Chief of *Kenya Studies Review,* a premier and interdisciplinary journal devoted to publishing contemporary scholarship on Kenya. Her passion is to empower young girls through her writing and believes when you empower girls, you empower a nation.

A SHOT OF HOPE

We've lived through it all, an unspoken trauma,
But braved it with aching hearts and tears
Though numbed by our daily losses: A dead child.
A dead brother. A dead sister. A dead mother.
A dead father. A dead grandfather. A dead grandmother.
A dead Wife. A dead husband. A friend. A neighbor!
Dead as a tree stump; all gone without fanfare or pomp,
—If ever fanfare and pomp exist in death—
From which every second. Every minute. Every hour—
Weeks and months on end—many have fallen prey to its
    clutches
This ceaseless plague with the markings of the Black Death,
Ravaging nations and leaving only devastation in its wake,
Alas, people turned into a dot on maps, too impersonal to bear
Making me wonder if the almighty had Her back from us turned,
Forcing our fate into the arms of science to be and live;
Yet, still left to drink the bitter dregs of our endless losses!

Today, a shot in the arm is our only hope and lifeline
A saving grace to reel ourselves and the world
From our uneasy fears of this unforgiving Black Death
To emerge from this deep sea of sorrow to see another dawn
Slowing down this derailed caboose of our lives
Today, I disrobe my arm with glee to the biting sting of steel
Hopeful it will tame this untamable airborne virus,
Hoping against hope that we would all, in due time,
Shine again against the gloom of our lived past gory
Be reunited with those from whom in months on end
A chasm of separation has existed to our heart's chagrin
And celebrate in our reunion with pomp and fanfare,
Giving COVID-19 virus its merited middle finger!

A FOLK IN THE ROAD

A folk in the road is all I need to find my footing again,
As I seek that precious less travelled road to live and be.
For I, like all humanity, have weathered many troublesome days,
Held prisoner in the belly of a heartless beast for months on
    end,
But still I cling onto science, my only ray of hope, for a new
    dawn
Trusting its shine will put an end to my endured hurt and
    sadness!
A shot in the arm is my yardstick to ascend into the healing light
Against COVID-19's ceaseless and merciless punishing hand,
Paving way for me to soar like incense to the sky with glee!

Yesterday, I got a shot in my arm and couldn't be happier!
Now, with the winds of my unfettered freedom within grasp,
My life, like of a newly released prisoner, feels blissfully strange
Not even the smiles of my hidden joy can tame my silent fears
That my heart's thrums still sound alarm bells of caution
Is true as panic pangs surge in the wake of my vaccination

That COVID-19's invisible threats still remain a cliffhanger
From which only the Almighty knows its foreseeable end!

ENDLESS

We've lived through this pandemic in sorrow, but still, we rise
We've endured its drag of forced separation, but still, we rise
We've seen too much death every day of the hour, but still, we
    rise
We've seen parking lots turned into morgues, but still, we rise
We've seen families weather the toll of their losses, but still,
    they rise
We've seen lives changed in a flash without notice, but still,
    they rise

And, amid it all, our enduring spirits linger on, clinging onto life
Aware hope can, like withered leaves, fall off in a twinkling
Yet, optimistic a stab in the arm will make us whole again
Not masked-up like masked ninjas in the wake of our days
So today, with eyes closed, I extended my hand in *its* receipt
A sweet stab no more painful than an insect bite to my skin
But soon fears crowd me, like it has others, as my heart races
Unsure of the outcome of my stabbing; for in my craven heart,
I know ill-fate is never too distant from me like the virus itself

Ivonne Gordon Carrera Andrade
(Quito, Ecuador)

Ivonne Gordon Carrera Andrade (Quito, Ecuador) is a widely anthologized international award-winning poet, literary critic, translator, and Professor of Latin American Literature at the University of Redlands. She has been the recipient of many international poetry awards: She has read twice at the Library of Congress, as well as at multiple international poetry festivals, and her work is part of more than twenty international anthologies and has been translated into English, Polish, Flemish, Romanian, and Greek. She holds a Ph.D. from the U. of California, Irvine.

THE RISE AND FALL

Nothing remains the same,
sunshine fades, snow melts away,
days go by, dawn goes to day,
paradise turns to grief.

Nothing stays the same.

Empires rise and fall, tyrants fall in disgrace.

Everything that goes up must come down.

Nothing stays.

Sunrise's hue so hard to hold,
the sound of silence so hard to listen.
Be still in the dance, travel into the woods,
they are dark and deep, they whisper
in our deaf ears songs of wonder,
they trap the breeze's dew,
they dance with lifted eyes counting the stars.
One clock of light against the sky counting the beams
of wonder.

Be still.

Nothing remains the same.

THE ART OF LOSING

It is not hard to lose oneself,
it takes a while to learn,
every day it is a good practice
to lose something,
learn it.

Things sometimes want to be lost,
that is why we put them in secure places
never to be found again.

It is an art to lose,
like the roses lose their aroma day after day,
the trees lose their leaves,
the birds lose their own after they learn to fly.

I know there is a condor inside waiting to fly away.

Jack Ogembo
(Kisii, Kenya)

Jack O. Ogembo is an Associate Professor of Literature at the University of Kabianga in Rift Valley Province but hails from Kisumu in Nyanza. He holds B. Ed, M. A in Lit, and Ph.D. in Lit degrees from the University of Nairobi, the City University of New York, and the University of Cape Town, respectively. His keen interest in theorizing literature motivated him to conduct his doctorate research on Art and Ethno-medicine among the Luos. The field data were rigorously subjected to the Body as Text theory. He has also published articles, short stories, and book chapters. He has taught literature at Moi, Maseno, and now Kabianga Universities.

THE TREE OF LIFE

Life without lies is untenable
For life is fused with death and death fused with life
Truth is hypocritically mounted on the pedestal,
But ubiquitous lies are worshipped in the dark
It is lies that run Statecraft and multinational companies
While the tree pickets the doctrine of classified information
Truth extended reflects rudiments of lies and when
Lies are interrogated; they display the fangs of truth.
Who can demarcate the boundary between the two?
For the borders keep shifting and instability, fragmentations
And transitions, change and endlessness, constitute their
    eternal hallmarks
Every truth and every lie are just but tentative as the best liar
    gets the gal
Prisons are teeming with innocent convicts, while freeways,
    highways,
And courtrooms (benches and bars) showcase the latest
    limousines
Owned by the free and smartest thieves!

The pulpits are manned by crooks and con men extorting
tithes and offerings from gullible public. The tree is a silent
    observer,
its leaves taking notes, the trunk raising points of order and the
    roots
chairing the meeting. Navigating life, so daunting that death
    would
constitute such a pleasant alternate destination. The duality
    between truth and lies
is such a mystery that researchers have been unable to
    disentangle it for eternity.
'Woe unto the generations that will live in the post truth era!'

Jane Beatrice Ovbude Ejim
(Tralee County Kerry, Republic of Ireland)

Jane Beatrice Ovbude Ejim is from Nigeria but resides in the Republic of Ireland. Jane is writer of short stories and poetry. She is an author of four books, her most popular book, *Halo life book of poetry*, has been literally adopted into a stage play in the Republic of Ireland. Jane Beatrice is a mother of three kids, who are currently pursuing their education at university level. She has an accounting background, trained in community development, and has a degree in Business marketing. She is currently pursuing a master's program in business management.

STAYING AND ROMANCING
WITH NATURE

Staying and romancing with nature
Use your hands when you can
Open the door and lift an object
Don't forget to kiss your fingers as you eat.

Staying and romancing with nature
Put your legs to work on daily bases
Match on the sand and step on stones
You will be healed and not hurt

Staying and romancing with nature
Don't backbite me or someone else
for the mouth and brain to keep busy
Chew the nuts and fruits
show someone a little kindness everyday day or two
and you will be glad that you did

Sweets and chocolates will send you to hell
But natural food will redeem you from pain
Positive thoughts always remain a medicine to the heart

Growing and understanding yourself
Use your eyes and let them see
A natural light from the sky every day
Observing the colors, of different shapes, and sizes
Let this intrigue you about other beings
As it does in every object around you

Staying and romancing with nature
Water, water, water is always a friend
On your skin on daily bases
Wash, wash, wash and not just to wipe

Drink natural water as much as you can
And it will bring healing to your body and soul.

The lesson cannot be compressed in words
slowing our spirit, no permission for a choice
we are forced to finally to sit , slow and appreciate

 staying and romancing with nature
 when good days are here again
we would be glad that we have space to breadth just as a team

THE COVID AND US

Is marriage a contract of financial insurance?
Is it a change of name for a woman created to migrate?
To some it became a master-slave attachment
Just to be christened 'sir, your food is ready'

This is no fiction, this is no drama
History may not capture as we lived it in real time
The joy in many, the violence and frustration in others

It is not possible 'we debated in politics and science
but didn't the earth clean itself in an overwhelming surprise?

telling you and I that after-all, life can buy what money cannot

This we behold in the ingenuity of our children
all they wanted was just a space, to play, and to laugh.

Jaydeep Sarangi
(Jhargram, West Bengal, India)

Jaydeep Sarangi is a poet with ten collections, translator, academic, and interviewer. He specializes in marginal studies, postcolonial discourse, and new poetry. Sarangi has produced several books and articles on Dalit writers and activists from India. He is a widely anthologized and reviewed bilingual poet with eight collections in English. He is the President of the Guild of Indian English Writers Editors and Critics (Kerala) and Vice President, Executive Council, IPPL, ICCR, Kolkata. He is a Principal and Professor involved in the poetry movement for social change anchored in Kolkata, India.

A LONELY EVENING IN KOLKATA

The day's colors move into memory
The white prides of the day
Settles into a dreamless sleep

As this torrid summer breeze sails over me
And my story begins and ends
The silent waters of the Ganges

Exhibit the dark magic of the past
Marx and Gandhi hold hands together
My lonely late moon rises.

The wishes take shape somewhere
In the evening's dark kingdom
My thoughts lead me to the river of hope, brimming.

TOMORROW

I return to muddy walls near the river
Erratic November rain heals the world.
Now my imagination is wet and green.

Night birds are carrying life pulse
Though our hearts have deep bloody wounds
Though the air if full of hatred and self-love
Erring weaves gather mud
Even then, the world is engrossed in dreams of the dawn.

Thoughts stay at night leading to the morning
Lonely birds find shelter in trusted homes
Their voice clears on trying to describe a sweet kiss.

Jim Landwehr
(Waukesha, Wisconsin, USA)

Jim Landwehr has three published memoirs. He also has five poetry collections. His nonfiction has been published in Main Street Rag, The Sun Magazine, and others. His poetry has been featured in Orchard Poetry Journal, Blue Heron Review and many others. He lives in Waukesha, Wisconsin with his wife and enjoys fishing, kayaking, biking and camping. Jim was the 2018-2019 poet laureate for the Village of Wales, Wisconsin.

TOMORROW'S PROMISES

I saw him on my morning walk
sitting on the steps of his home
waiting for the school bus
backpack at his feet
mask on his face

We are all in this pandemic together
but for some reason
every time I see a young student
wearing a mask
I get terribly sad

These children are just getting started
their lives lay before them
stretching to the horizon
of what seems like a flat world
ever since COVID-19 showed up

But we are a resilient species
and with young innovators
looking toward the sun
and not the pits of darkness
we shall march toward "better"

Our isolation has been a time of
introspection, adjustment
mourning and dreaming
thinking of how life once was
in the old days of last year

With vaccines on the scene
our despair turns to hope
masks hide our smiles of relief

at the promise of normalcy
approaching like a distant train

One day this will be a distant dream
when we arrive there we must never take
hugging and handshakes for granted
but rather embrace one another
like it could be the last time

PARENTING A PANDEMIC

I liken coming out of covid
a bit to the parenting process
the difference being
months instead of years

As parents we spend years
in trenches with the burdens
of diapers, naps and storytime
day care, school and runny noses

With covid it was months of masks
disinfectant, two-meter perimeters
plexiglas, cancelled events
and long hours confined at home

Parenting is done out of duty and love
a planned, coordinated experience,
difficult as it was
with an outcome that pays dividends

Covid living is founded in fear
an unexpected lifestyle disruption
requiring selflessness and sacrifice
the only result being life as it was.

When the children grew up
it was like we surfaced from drowning.
Whereas news of a vaccine
provides a momentary cleansing breath

Joan McNerney
(Ravena, New York, USA)

Joan McNerney, originally from Brooklyn, now resides in Ravena, a small town near Albany, New York. She has been the recipient of three scholarships. Most of her professional background was spent in the advertising business. She has recited her work at the National Arts Club, New York City, State University of New York, Oneonta, McNay Art Institute, San Antonio and the University of Houston, Texas as well as other distinguished venues. Her poetry has been included in numerous literary magazines and she has been nominated four times for *Best of the Net*. Her poems are about spring which is a time of hope and happiness here in the northeast section of the United States.

A GLIMPSE OF SPRING

shy blue morning
black trees etch sky

children skipping
over puddles

bramble on snow
soft birdsong

listening to water
race downstream

winds gently kiss
my forehead

grass shoots push
through first thaw

TREES OF HEAVEN

Those are tough trees
 growing in slums.

With no need for rich soil
or pruning, they rise
in abandoned lots.

Trees that survive
rubbish, rodents
noxious chemicals.

Not easily cut down,
they stand against
gaunt tenements.

Climbing skyward,
delicate palm leaves
flourish flowering pods.

Trees of Heaven give
children glimpses of bright
emerald each morning.

Stars play peek-a-boo
between their branches
through long nights.

Who has said a taste of
paradise is only for the rich?

John Curl
(Berkeley, California, USA)

John Curl is the author of twelve books of poetry, including Revolutionary Alchemy and Yoga Sutras of Fidel Castro; his translations of Inca, Maya, and Aztec poets are collected in Ancient American Poets. He represented the USA at the World Poetry Festival in Venezuela, and lives in Berkeley, California. He is a member of the Revolutionary Poets Brigade of San Francisco.

RAINBOW WEATHER

Dueling with the devil
In the eye of the hurricane,
Venus in retrograde
Aries rising,
dark spots cover the sun,
predators without shame,
nothing true under their darkness,
nothing new under their guns.
nothing to eat but
dogsbane and wolfsbane,
nothing to cast but blame,
nothing can change without
struggle and pain,
but nothing can stay the same.

But those murmurs in the gales
gusting all around us
sing of something
just beyond the storm:
rainbow weather's rolling in,
I can smell it, I swear it,
rainbow weather's rolling in like dawn.

Armies marching through the night,
monumental crimes and blunders,
scorched cliffs all around us,
centuries of rape and plunder,
bats flocking together
centipedes abusing power
jackals sniffing every crack
for lovers in a secret bower.

But those murmurs in the gales

gusting all around us
sing of something
just beyond the storm:
rainbow weather's rolling in,
I can smell it, I swear it,
rainbow weather's rolling in like dawn.

John Tunaley
(Manchester, England, UK)

John Tunaley was born in Manchester, England, in 1945 and had been writing for over sixty years with a cardboard box full of loose yellowing manuscripts to prove it. He now lives in North Yorkshire, where he writes with two groups. He likes anthologies and feels safe in them, possibly because he grew up in a terraced house. Although oddly enough, he hates being pigeonholed. Recently a friend said they liked his poems… "they are sort of higgledy-piggledy but leave strong images"…Praise indeed…Modesty forbids more.

UNDERPASS ON THE A34

From Journal of a Plague Year
Perry Barr Underpass,
Birmingham, 06.01.2021

In a world that's full of fractured paving
it is necessary to go carefully…
…watch your step as the demons balefully
wait for the slightest sign of quavering…
(The smoke advances… the forest retreats
before the holocaust of settlements…)
The planets' frittered wealth forms sediments
in the underpass. Once the traffic beats
it to a pulp, the sacred seed falls…
…there it sprouts without complaining…. indeed
it rises full of grace. Whether weed
or wheat… fruit or thorn, the concrete walls
are softened … ennobled…as the vegetation
reaches for the light in clear, joyous, attention…

LES DENTS-DE-LION

From The Third Programme
Old St Stephen Church, Robin Hood's Bay
01/12/2020)

Weeded with a military precision
gone mad, the lines between the paving stones
gaped as black as a Rauschenberg painting.
The dandelions held their nerve…feigning
death for a week or two. Now look again.
Small, circled fans of toothed leaves have regained
their rightful place. Springing from deep tap-roots,
the flowers aim and prepare to shoot.

They're not dismayed by December weather
but will bide their time …sit quietly tethered
in their cracks. Arrange themselves in mannered
ranks…check the diary and next year's planner…
…gather their forces…defy man's foul corrections…
and come early April, stage some resurrections …

Joseph A. Farina
(Sarnia, Ontario, Canada)

Joseph A. Farina is a retired lawyer in Sarnia, Ontario, Canada. He has had two books of poetry published—The Cancer Chronicles and The Ghosts of Water Street. Several of his poems have been published in different Magazines and appears in anthologies.

THIS TOO SHALL PASSOVER

this is not our last supper
the circumstances of our suffering
will not end our gatherings

the hunger for light and hallelujahs
undiminished in this universe

we shall increase with dividends
by the sensations of the heart

impercetively in all seasons
until the inexorable law
of diminishing returns retreats

RESPITE

the sunlight streams through the winter-stained windows. warm,
yellow rivulets of light casting ciarroscuro points throughout
the kitchen. a throwback to those youthful Kellogg cornflakes
mornings. everything gilded in amber and white embracing
housebound plants hungry for its caresses.an early promise of its
future returns, an early laying of its healing hands upon we
winter covid weary.

BEGINNINGS

become the street this night
meld with the voices from shadows
in harmony under streetlights
listen to new songs written
across a nation of avenues
become the saxophonist
alone at a window in Harlem
become the strings of flamenco
guitars in Miami Barrios
alleluias sound by gospel choirs
let your heart cry to its sorrow
we are all beloved of someone lost
destroy the dark fears with love
the street calls to us this night
joined by its thought of journing
across the nation of grace
from its dawning to its sunset

Julio Cesar Paz
(Cienfuegos, Cuba)

Julio César Paz is a Cuban, born and raised in a small city by the beach. He has always been in love with the sea; the dancing of the waves is his quiet place. Majored in language education in 2011, Julio has taught literature in different universities in Cuba. He loves reading and writing, and prefers to read in the original language. About a year ago, he decided to travel around the world to learn from different cultures. There was no specific destination; he went where the tides took him. Currently, Julio is living and working as a literature teacher in Hanoi, Vietnam.

PERHAPS, MY CAT

waking up to three chargers on my bed was a good sign. still
attached to reality. though my cat cannot really appreciate my
faith, he takes a leap every time. Purr

HABANERAS (ODES)

out of her name, I only keep
the short vowels and the long
moans

I could forget
but
the insane tendency of your lips biting the sand
at dawn before the rain.

It was just
the beach and
your cold-blooded
lips

on my neck
announcing

a new storm.

Kahtan Mandwee
(Rochester, Michigan, USA)

Poet, novelist, translator, Kahtan Mandwee wrote two novels, two memoires, and ten volumes of poetry in English and Arabic. Professor Mandwee holds a B.A., M.A., and Ph.D. in English literature and creative writing and has been teaching for forty years.

ROSES AND CANARIES

Rochester Hills, MI, 31 May 2021

My house is whiter than the cotton empires of the Mississippi.
I gather my verses, memories, in a tiny canoe, ready to depart.
Late April snowstorms wither the burgeoning, delicate daisies
    and tulips.
Thunder, lightning, heavy rains improvise over my decayed roof.
Yearning for sunrays, missing autumn, I ardently listen to wild
    winds,
losing my presence to sweet melodies,
of canaries, nesting on maples, climber rosebushes,
shading my front window and porch, nostalgically greeting my
    sight.
The lush grass, yawning, impatiently waits for a trim.
The apple, fig, peach, and apricot trees are budding, surrounding
    the yard.
I joyfully whisper:
Corona is almost dead,
let us celebrate this paradise,
sing with the canaries and the butterflies
to liberty, justice, and love.

MADRID WITHOUT YOU

To late Iraqi poet Abd Al-Wahab Al-Bayatti
Madrid, Spain, June 2013

For three long days,
I roamed the crowded streets of Madrid,
gazing at the lonely faces of strangers, sitting in cafés,
searching for your kind, peaceful eyes.
I couldn't find you or the café where we sat,
in the late afternoon, of a summer day,
chatting of Baghdad, myrtles, and poets,
reciting verses, plagiarizing metaphors
from the wide, chestnut eyes of gorgeous Spanish girls.
After three, poignant, forlorn decades
of sorrow, war, and oblivion,
long dead and gone,
why did I see your face
in the face
of every human
I met?

GODDESS

To Muntaha
7:20 A.M. Saturday, October 5th, 2013

In the midst of my insomniac, barren nights,
I recall your sleepy, bereaved eyes
flooding profusely, like monsoon rains,
on your gardenia cheeks.
That day, we kissed, hugged, and departed,
never to meet again.
You were a pretty girl I devotedly worshipped like Ishtar.*
Four bitter-sweet decades of war, death, and exile
haven't distorted your image or love.
You remained a demigod
in the figure of a young girl,
I lunatically adored,
and still tearfully idolize,
remember, and weep.

---

* Ishtar is the goddess of love and fertility in the Sumerian mythology.

Adolescent Love

To N. H
Rochester Hills, February 2019

For I tearfully adored you and agonizingly starved for your
    warmth,
I long for you now, my yearning for Iraq's dates.
Reminiscing, whenever exile drags me down,
frost gnaws my toes and bones, desolation carries me over a
    dolphin's wing,
I languish for the shine of your eyes, the softness of your touch,
the innocence of your soul.

Your face is a full moon; sweet are your luring lips.
Forlorn, grieving, wounded by the dagger of despair,
searching among the empty shells for the pearls and nectars of
    youth,
the abject scent of myrtles, your touch,
I espy you consoling my tears, sharing the murmurs of my veins,
unveiling a narrow hole through which I enter a delirious world,
    drowning in stars.

Now, here, perplexed, loveless, reminiscing,
the joy of nightingales brings me to tears.
Iraq dwells and moans in my blood.

Longing for its redolent, datepalms' pollen,
I yearn and desire you.

Returning to these tranquil shores,
the adolescence's fire dances in our laps, around us

as we bend and circle after its flames,
while the sweet Tigris
runs for us,
only for us,
under the trillion stars,
in the tender night.

Karlo Sevilla
(Quezon City, Philippines)

Karlo Sevilla of Quezon City, Philippines is the author of the full-length poetry collection, "Metro Manila Mammal" (Some Publishing, 2018), and two chapbooks. Recognized among the Best of Kitaab 2018 and shortlisted for the Oxford Brookes International Poetry Competition 2021, his poems appear in *Philippines Graphic, Sub-Saharan Magazine, Communicators League, DIAGRAM, Protean*, and elsewhere.

MORTALS, WE

Hubris is fleeting fire;
real fires can kill us --
unfiguratively, unmetaphorically.

Isn't it romantic to declare
we'll die fighting?

As if every breath
and utterance
is a battle cry,
when we
just die.

There are forces much greater than us;
we are insignificant motes of dust,
prey to conquests and cycles
of days and nights,
good and evil.

We are more mere than more,
but we'll grittily fight our fade,
won't we?

Or gracefully dance
our ephemerality
away...

I PROMISE WHAT I CAN'T DELIVER

Amidst all this madness,
let this be your reprieve:
Believe when I say,
I'll take you to where
tenderness reigns supreme,
and the times we exert strength,
it is only to love and dance.

There, all the little children
grow up and well,
gain knowledge except
on how to exploit one another,
advance in years until met
by peaceful death.

Believe what I myself
don't believe,
because it's still worth
the prize:

What for a moment lies
behind your moist eyes.

Kate Young
(Chatham, Kent, UK)

Kate Young lives in England and has been passionate about poetry since childhood. Her poems have appeared in Ekphrastic Review, The Poetry Village, Words for the Wild, Poetry on the Lake, Alchemy Spoon, Dreich and The Poet. She has had poems in two Scottish Writers Centre chapbooks. Her work has also featured in the anthologies Places of Poetry and Write Out Loud. Her pamphlet *A Spark in the Darkness* has been published by Hedgehog Press.

THE UNFOLDING

Freedom Day, July 19, 2021

it was the year of the two-dimensional,
months caught in the stutter-freeze
of a screen, the anxious wait
as an unstable connection
threatened to truncate the link

to loved ones, their faces
folded safely in pockets,
each crease chosen with care
to avoid the decapitation of a smile,
or smooth skin that smelled of ink

but now the unfolding begins

newly grown into the frown
that she was born with,
her dimpled limbs wriggle free
and reach towards me, a stranger
my joyous face escaping the mask

I hold the weight of her, letting
fullness settle in the ease of my lap
and inhale her baby-milk-scent,
listen to the contented slip-slurp sounds
layered with bouts of howling lungs

now filling the room with life

Kathleen Herrmann
(Vallejo, California, USA)

Kathleen Herrmann has published poems and non-fiction articles and has written song lyrics which she accompanies on ukulele. She has taught young writers since 1998, who in turn, awaken her own inner child. Outdoor adventures, people, current events, and unexpected happenings inspire her writing, as well as the evocative poetry, prose, storytelling and oral improvisation of fellow authors.

SING OUT LOUD

I.
Almost March
Stippled sunlight streaks damp stones
Sharp green edges slice soil and bark
Tender buds swell pastel
Blushing dots and bold dashes
Exposed to naked eye

Four patio chairs
Warming bowls of chili
So much to say
Across still necessary gap

Listen
Pear tree
Top tier

Smooth high whistle
Crisp trill
Husky alto upslur
Shrill "ree-bee-oos"
Mechanical drone
Fluted grace notes
Melodic solo
Lush ensemble

Feathered Ellas brazen and full-throated
Broadcast deep-down song
Ethereal chorus rings
Shattering winter's hush
Arise weary warriors
Sing!
Sing out loud!

II.
Another day
Quarantined
Working online angles
Snag a vaccine

Big blue text
Splashes screen
Remember me?
Alto--Messiah '19
We were too hot to Handel
You, Peg and me
Blended close harmony

Here's my little fantasy
Sing again
Swing again
Just us three

Breath catches
Endorphins rush
Fingers can't fly fast enough

Indigo house
Quiet street
Uh one, two, three, four
Tapping feet

Open window
Welcome song
Dormant murmurs
Rise up strong

Last beat
Eyes meet
We're back
So sweet
You, Peg and me
Blended close harmony

Kay Ritchie
(Glasgow, Scotland, UK)

Kay Ritchie grew up in Glasgow and Edinburgh, lived in London, Spain, and Portugal, and worked as a freelance photographer and radio producer. She has been published in numerous anthologies and has performed at various events. She enjoys dancing and walking. In 2019 she walked the Camino Santiago Compostela and next year hopes to walk the Hebridean Way, across ten Scottish islands.

THE UNLOCKING

as if emerging
dust-encrusted
from some fur-lined
dank & wormy
underground
our fingernails torn & worn
from scrabbling for daylight
below clay and earth
above rebirth &
wingless
weightless
as Boticelli's Venus
balloon-buoyed
we will float…float
like dust motes
balanced on a scallop shell
before we're hurtled back
towards the ground

CHINK OF LIGHT

scraped scoured scrubbed
by 'the wire brush of doubt'
throughout this pandemic
emotions caked
like dried up food
over cooked
bottom-burnt
left-overs layers & lumps
looking for answers
how much longer with
the heat turned up too high
waiting to come off the boil
waiting
waiting
till 'time comes good'

Ketaki Datta
(Kolkata, India)

Ketaki Datta is an Associate Professor of English at Bidhannagar Government College, Kolkata, India. She did her Ph.D. on Tennessee Williams's late plays, later published titled Black and Non-Black Shades of Tennessee Williams. She has quite a few academic publications, two novels, two books of poems, and quite a few translations. Her short stories have been published in different anthologies and online journals. She is a regular reviewer of poetry volumes with Compulsive Reader, USA, and the Regional Editor, India, of "thetheatertimes.com."

IN A CORONA-FREE WORLD

The strange pathogen has beaten a retreat at last!
Though soothsayers say, another wave may come
But when we know not, next month or January first,
We keep our fingers crossed and ourselves mum!

But now I am planning a trip to the hills,
A journey to the South may be,
Hills and greenery, murmuring trills
Though attract me more, there I wannabe!

Corona fear shoved me indoors,
Compelled me to do boring chores,
Now I shall surely allow my mind
To follow a brand-new course!

Hey Covid-19, enough is enough
Why don't you breathe your last?
You took terrible toll of innocent lives
Now you should be a thing of the past!

Now we must go to the shopping malls
To the opera-house, to ice-cream parlors,
Now let's stay outdoors, frequent movie-halls
Cruise in a lake or sail off to harbors.

The quiet desolate roads are now
Teeming with passersby, with jaywalkers,
The silent taverns are chock-a-block now
With boozing youths, regular customers!

Peep into the bistros or into the eateries
No seat lies vacant, the waiters are busy
Plying orders, listening to foodies—
Life is now becoming normal and easy!

Corona, hey you evil incarnate
We dislike having you with us,
Your vindictive return we hate,
Vanish forever or gently pass!

Dreaming of Post-Covid World in the times of Corona

Loneliness inside the room
Spread its legs, lay on one side,
Tossed and turned,
Talked to its own shadow,
Counted the gables twice,
Thrice, even more.

Spider's webs proliferated,
Blowing out of proportions,
Oh! Alack! What a pity!
The shaggy brush, thrust it
Away, tore it asunder!
The spider ran helter-skelter,
Rendered homeless, with
No chance to weave a cobweb
In a month or two.

The charwoman had melted
into thin air—
The mop-brush, the broomstick
All stirred in the room,
Where dust meant a
nonexistent speck now,
Where they all were keen
on beating loneliness,
boredom, uncertainty!

They all dreamt of a thoroughfare
Chock-a-block with black heads,
White blazers and green saris!

They all dreamt of a market
Which roomed jostling throngs
Of crossings, teeming with
flurry of footfalls,
and honking cabs!

They awaited a dawn in bated breath,
which will usher in
A new world, labelled as 'post-Covid',
Healthy, sick-and-span, very vivid!

Laksmisree Banerjee
(Ashiana Gardens, Jamshedpur, Jharkhand, India)

Laksmisree Banerjee is an established Poet, Writer, Editor, Literary Critic, practicing Vocalist, and Educationist with many National and International Publications and Awards to her credit. She has eight published books of poetry, with one hundred twenty research publications in Journals, Anthologies across the world with several Academic Books. She is a Senior Fulbright Scholar and Professor (USA), Commonwealth Scholar (UK), National Scholar & Gold Medalist of Calcutta University, India, UGC Post-Doctoral Research Awardee, and Ex Vice Chancellor of Kolhan University, the largest in Jharkhand, India.

RHYME OF LIFE

Let us meet after pandemic times
Let us meet in victorious climes

Let us meet after the virus is dead
Let us meet in the sunny green spread

Let us meet after dark sorrows end
Let us meet in happiness round the bend

Let us meet in the warmth of our palm
Let us meet in the sunrise of joyous calm

Let us meet when science is cherished
Let us meet when death is vanquished

Let us meet as we often did in the past
In health, wealth and merry realms vast

OUR GLEAMING PLANET

This speck of life
  This mote of dust
    From the elements
      To my effervescent me
Seems to waver, quiver, invigorate
  In the cuddle of my genial palms
In the beating of my cherry-rose heart
  So intangibly tied in gossamer strings
With the aureoles and cosmic heavings—

Life that magical pied piper
  Ever treacherous
    Ever scintillating
      Fights with my perennial love
Yet serenades the magic song
  Of bonding in our cupola
    Never ever lasting as we thought it was
Still an infinite rhyme beyond the ephemera—

So let us hug, dance, love, live and sing
  Keep the sequined midnight reveling
In the perfumed breeze heralding sunrise
  Let us keep this fairy song ceaseless, pulsating
With the breath of our ambrosial being
  The divine eternities we already snuggle
Preserved within our soul-interstices—

We disseminate this vibrant love and life
  Through ether, land, water of our glad earth
    In every particle, bloom, minuscule firefly
As blithe butterflies we dance in honey-gardens
  Through the sunny arches of the nectarine air and skies
    Across the pink blushing cheeks of the horizon—

Till God descends to vitalize our desiccated desert
    And transform the grey spectral mirage
Into our dazzling ocean of love-laden life
    So we may stop, live, think, in the sunrise revive
In this hospitable home of ours, our elemental bee-hive—

MORNING OF HOPE

The sun is rising slowly
but steadily
with its orbed crowning glory
soothing in its orange pulpy story
our nature's rotund fruit
of gleaming succulence
calming the turbulent seas
of aching strife,
of ruddy pain and angry blight.

Soon the sparkling aura
of the caressing new sun
makes us dance in fresh light
till the grey dismal night is erased
with a whiff of perfumed breeze
and halo blithe,
as we merry-make in animation
with our rekindled Love and Life.

Lee Kuei-shien
(Taipei, Taiwan)

Lee Kuei-shien was born in Taiwan in 1937, a retired Chairman of the National Culture & Arts Foundation in Taiwan, and now the vice president of Movimiento Poetas del Mundo founded in Chile in 2005. He has published 53 poetry books in different languages. In addition to Taiwan, his achievement in poetry creation has been awarded internationally in India, Mongolia, Korea, Bangladesh, Macedonia, Peru, Montenegro and Serbia so far.

THE LUCE CHAPEL

In early morning
the clock
still sleeps peacefully.
There is a voice from afar
leading me to here.
I turn back in front of the clock tower
finding you with two hands meeting together
in praying toward heaven.
Among the clouds
a trace of morning glory
shines on
your fingertips.
I desire to lie on the green land
around you
as my eternal bed.

CLIMBING UP THE HILLTOP IN KEELUNG

Along Rongxuan Trail in Keelung
I walk on the stone steps in early morning
expecting to find better scenery at higher level.
Among the dense leaves of a big banyan
with fibrous roots growing down to reach the earth
the chorus of birds begins to sing in a symphony.
The weeds and wildflowers beckon me along the path.
I look up and find the white clouds in smiling
to inspire me a poetic feeling in my mind
after the baptism with long windy rainy days.
The stone steps in meandering
lead me going up and up
until the viewing platform on the hilltop.
Overlooking the magnificent ocean
which displays the strong spirit of surfing waves
and the turbulent currents against the distant challenges
I stand independently in silence at the hilltop
and feel wholeheartedly my homeland of Taiwan island
staying alone between heaven and earth proudly.

Les Wicks
(Mortdale, NSW, Australia)

Over 45 years Wicks has performed widely across Australia and internationally. Published in over 400 different magazines, anthologies & newspapers across 36 countries in 15 languages. Edited a number of projects, the most recent publication is *Guide to Sydney Crime* (2022).
His 15th book of poetry is *Time Taken – New & Selected* (Puncher & Wattmann, 2022).

AT THE ROUND TABLE

Alice mentions *God*, a drop tone & volume
like referring to some friend that deserted us,
the disgrace
that irrelevance.
Mark mentions *Water* like some horndog—
his uncritical appetite is applauded,
some folks like the familiarities of lechers
even if focused on dirt & trees.
It's something close to *Certainty*.

Shake the rattles, my bongo is bung
there's got to be music.
Outside a storm is rolling in from Liverpool,
currawongs & lorikeets are frantic.

My life is no European car…
perhaps a serviceable bicycle
with LED backlights.

Sweet, aging brain. Untrustworthy eyes—
Gaia totters towards a turning.
Some gang we are!
Professional bailers in Atlantis,
wherever we sit there is beauty.
Our ambitious seagrass eyebrows rise
towards even the suggestion of light—
we are rooted in the ocean sediments
and thrive.

Linda M. Crate
(Meadville, Pensylvania, USA)

Linda M. Crate's works have been published in numerous magazines and anthologies both online and in print. She is the author of six poetry chapbooks the latest of which is *The Samurai* (Yellow Arrow Publishing, October 2020). She's also the author of the novel *Phoenix Tears* (Czykmate Books, June 2018). Recently she has published two full-length poetry collections, *Vampire Daughter* and *The Sweetest Blood*.

READY TO KNOW MY WILDNESS

i am ready to bloom again,
to grow past all these complications
and taste the sweet fragrance
that life can bring;
i ready to remember the softness
of petals and the caress of the breeze—

ready to see the rainbow that
comes after these dark storms,
and everything after that pot of gold;

every jewel of rain caught on the branches
of trees and every laughing crow—

i am ready to dive into the creek,
and let that water whisper to me all the secrets
of old and new;
cutting lose all the things that were cutting me

i am ready to know the wisdom and songs
of the trees—

ready to smell the forest,
taste the wild sweet air,
and witness the red capped mushrooms and
ferns growing in the woods;

i am ready to know my wildness once more.

i will believe in peace and flowers

as the dark nightmare
seems to becoming
closer to being just a black spot
in the rear view mirror

i am sure there will be
other dark dreams and scares,

but i will hold onto the
flower of hope in my heart
which never withers
no matter the circumstances;

and i will believe in peace and flowers—

i will believe in the song of birds,
the smell of the forest,
laughter of creeks and babbling brooks;

i will walk through flowers and grass and trees
without fear or the shadow of menance breathing down my
neck—

i will grow
out my roots again,
and feel the soft petals i forgot;
i will embrace birdsong nesting in my ears.

Lorraine Garnett
(Jamaica, West Indies)

Lorraine Garnett is a nanny in Brooklyn. She has previously worked as a preschool teacher, after school supervisor, and summer camp activities director. She is a member of PEN America, Worker Writers School, founded and directed by Mark Nowak. Her poems are forthcoming in several anthologies. Born and raised in Jamaica, Garnett currently lives in Brooklyn, New York.

LUCIFER GOT THE VACCINE

Lucifer got the vaccine, double dose—with no adverse reactions
not even a tic, nor overt or covert bias
After a year of whistling ambulances, ambulances with burnt
    exhaust
systems. Systems blowing heavy black fumes, systems coughing
    up smoke, speeding up and down deserted streets. Systems
    crying high pitched white noise
noise so frequent, sirens now turned into everyone's ringtones.

After a year of vanishing bodies—two, three, four generations,
    exiting without a choice. Generations after generations,
    disappearing right after gut-wrenching
FaceTime goodbyes. Generations silent by the ominous
    midnight virus.
Lucifer got the vaccine

After a year of hell, the devil must and will disappear
vaccines are here to stay. Lucifer got the vaccine
After a year of crippling pain, church bells will be ringing
families, friends, and foes will be singing. Airport security will be
    nodding
Vaccines are here to stay

After a year of solitude, our neighbors' touch is a promise.
Hearts will cartwheel its way to Broadway shows, to indoor,
    outdoor dining
Ice cream trucks will replace the unwanted piercing sirens
Hearts will cartwheel its way to museums, cartwheel its way to
    children's laughter, cartwheel its way to school openings and
    merry music festivals
cartwheel its way to grandma and grandpa's longing loving arms.
Vaccines are here to stay

After a year of isolation we are going to see, smell and touch the
    cherry blossoms.
see smell and touch tulips and daffodils
Hip hip hooray! Happy birthday! Happy birthday to us!
Lucifer got the vaccine! What a devil!

Lucille Lang Day
(Oakland, California, USA)

Lucille Lang Day is the award-winning author of four poetry chapbooks and seven full-length poetry collections, most recently *Birds of San Pancho and Other Poems of Place*. She has also published two children's books and a memoir, edited the anthology *Poetry and Science: Writing Our Way to Discovery*, and coedited *Fire and Rain: Ecopoetry of California* and *Red Indian Road West: Native American Poetry from California*. She is the founder and publisher of a small press, Scarlet Tanager Books, and lives in Oakland, California, with her husband, journalist and author Richard Michael Levine

I AM GLAD

that the Coffee Mill on Grand Avenue
was open the morning
my coffee maker stopped working

that the plumber was able to open
my clogged bathroom drain
and the kitchen light that stopped working
only needed a new bulb

that my husband and I have been
vaccinated against the coronavirus
and can now hug our grandchildren

that California poppies are lifting
their orange cups to the sun
along the edge of San Francisco Bay

that my neighbors have set up
a food pantry where hungry people
can get food for free

that we have a Native American
Secretary of the Interior
who wants to protect sacred lands

that a white police officer
has been convicted of murder for kneeling
on a Black man's neck until he died

that there is always change
allowing the unexpected
the whales returning from near extinction
the drought interrupted by rain

Marcelo Sánchez
(Frankfurt am Main, Germany)

Marcelo Sánchez is Argentine. He writes poems, short stories and essays. He currently lives in Germany.

BEAUTY

Based on etchings from
the Beauty series by Alex Katz

In one of my coronawanderings
I got to an art gallery,
a stone's throw from the Frankfurter Dom.
In one display window should still hang
four black and white etchings
of women's faces. (Alex Katz, isn't it?,
I said to myself in shock.) They happened
to be part of a larger portfolio.
I don't know why I come back every day
to that same window. (Or to that other
one with a copy of another female
bust, that of Nefertiti.)
Maybe I need the vigor
of the marks, the permanence
in forms that could shift any minute,
the light vibrating on the skin,
on hairdos and accessories. A sense
of Beauty give us all these beautiful
ladies. Another one, a real one,
is to inspire the next print.

A PANDEMIC

Try to remember what you used to feel.
These memories are the warmest part that's left
of all the experiences you've ever had,
of what you used to do in those old days.

I'm coughing for the first time this mild winter.
It doesn't matter that the doctor says:
Take some cough drops and turn the heater on.
You doubt it's the same coughing of past years.

I'm here. You're there. We never get to be
in the same place nor breath the common air.
Or is it that you're starting to forget?

Is the pandemic like another world?
It's a world that this early in the winter
continues to invade our little lives.

.

Mare Leonard
(City, Country)

Mare Leonard lives and works in the Hudson Valley where she is an Associate of the Institute for Writing and Thinking and the MAT programs at Bard College. She has published chapbooks and *The Dark Inside My Hooded Coat* was published *at* Finishing Line Press. She has published in *Ariel Chart, Bindweed,* and *Terror House* most recently. Finally she was nominated for a pushcart n 2018 for a poem in *The Pickled Body.*

INDEX

For resilience in the time of Covid-19
A Action, walk
B Believe in life
C Call a friend
D dust yes dust
E Elevate your feet
F forget past insults
G Give someone your time
H hang onto a sweet dream
I Initiate a Face time call
J Join a Zoom aerobics class
K Call the grand kids or any kid
L Love everyone but social distance
O OH say it scream it let go
M March around the house stomp it out
N Noise scream out the window bang a door
O open your lungs, breathe in 5 out 6
P Pick up the book yes read *His Only Wife*
S Stretch your toes to the ceiling lie down first
Q Question what you once believed, let it go
U With a friend, Unwind with a glass or two
V Variety: Thai, Japanese, Campbell's soup
W make al list of your Wishes
X Exit, left right or any direction you need to believe
Y not call a friend you haven't seen in years or more
Z Zone out once a day. do not feel guilty to dream

Mark Fleisher
(Albuquerque, New Mexico, USA)

Mark Fleisher's writings have taken him around the world as his work has appeared in numerous online and print anthologies in the United States, Canada, the United Kingdom, Kenya, Nigeria, South Africa, and India. Now living in Albuquerque, New Mexico, he has published three books of poetry (with prose and photographs added) and collaborated on a fourth volume. He is a member of the New Mexico State Poetry Society. A native of Brooklyn, New York, Fleisher earned a journalism degree from Ohio University and worked as a reporter and editor in upstate New York and Washington, D.C.

THINKING AHEAD TO TOMORROW

We are told it is
always darkest
before the dawn
These many months
we thought ahead
to tomorrow when
we might emerge from
darkness into light
free from shadows
obscuring our hopes

New leaders of my
country replenish
my reservoir of hope,
leaders who do not
disdain science
nor mock opponents
nor ignore the underserved

We welcome life when
the restart button
is pushed after
our long pause
but remain wary
of this new normal
for we are cautioned
the virus may never
fully be eradicated

Yes, I want to attend
concerts, enjoy theater,
cheer at an athletic event
Yes, I want to hug again,

see friends in person,
not on a computer screen,
shake hands, not elbow bump

Be patient, I tell myself

My heart wants so much
yet my head counsels
against expectations
too lofty for reality
my head a deterrent
against arrogance
fueled by complacency
birthed by vaccines
my head a brake
on unfettered optimism

People who know about
these things tell me
mask wearing must continue
how long no one can say;
I can do this—a small price
to pay for the beam of light
arriving with tomorrow

M Chambers
(Guisborough, North East England, UK)

M Chambers started writing at School, but even at an earlier age (8-9), he used to make up stories on family holidays about the area they were staying in and the landscape. He attended University College, Durham, obtaining his BA in 1987 and, in 1994, his Ph.D. in the archaeology and architecture of Durham Castle. He started working as a professional archaeologist and spent nearly 30 years working around the country. He wrote in his leisure time and was the runner-up in a Short Story competition at his workplace. His short stories have won prizes. He is now retired and lives on the edge of the North York Moors.

JOURNEY OUT OF DARKNESS

Emerging from my shell,
A seed pushing green, through the mud of isolation.
Breaking out chrysalis-like.
Stretching my wings painfully,
waiting for the blood to flow.
Slowly I trudged up the hill.
Met the night worker coming down with his dog.
2020 a long shift for all of us;
No reward for overtime.
The icy wind across the moorland left no mark,
so numb had I become, to life in the shadows.

I descended gentle,
exploring this new world, carefully.
The liquid river-voice caressed the gravel on the road,
mingling with the hopeful song of the hedge.
The first fingers of the Sun stole over the leaves,
striking the weary houses.
Changing their concrete paths, Midas-like,
into rivers of gold.

The long night was passing.
An expectation in the very air.
The Light of Life returning, only needing a messenger.
The Robin flew down in crimson glory.
Self-important as a politician, before the cameras of the Press.
Looked up and down the road,
Glanced at me, and
announced the coming Day.

Miguel Ángel Olivé Iglesias
(Holguín, Cuba)

Miguel Ángel Olivé Iglesias. Cuba. Author, Poet, Writer, Essayist, Editor, Translator. Canada Cuba Literary Alliance (CCLA) President on the Cuban side. Editor-in-chief of The Ambassador magazine and Assistant Editor of The Envoy newsletter. Associate Professor with a Bachelor's degree in Education, a Major in English, and a Master's degree in Pedagogical Sciences. He has written and published numerous academic papers in Cuba, Mexico, Spain, and Canada, chiefly on foreign language teaching. His studies also focus on Canadian poetry and prose, publishing literary reviews.

SHELTER

Revised version.
The original one published in The Envoy 101,
Newsletter of the Canada Cuba Literary Alliance.
August, 2020
"That even as we hurt, we hoped."
Amanda Gorman

When we look around in these COVID days
we see insecurity, rush, shortages, blind alleys
and feel our world is coming to an end
but we must look around again
must find shelter in our families
in our friends, in the things we love and live for
and notice how they shine a light upon us, upon a life
that won't be uncertain forever.
We must look around—and up,
see the higher light above
see a smile and blessings descend onto us
and give us hope
for a better, brighter tomorrow.

I'll Face my Life Today
Though I walk in the valley of the shadow
of death I shall not fear. Psalms 23:4

I'll face my life today, my heart armored
with braveness, understanding, fortitude.
Challenges met,
light cast upon obscurity.
I'll walk in confidence towards uncertainty
to defeat it, a truthful
sleight of hand to overturn weakness of faith.
I'll serve a higher cause, as should be done.
My life the vessel, my heart
the perfect sail.

TUNNELING THROUGH THE MIST

Revised version.
The original one published
in the international anthology
In Silence We Wait. Hidden Brook Press. 2021
February 1, 2021

I am bound for Holguín from my hometown of Bayamo,
in a purring as-good-as-brand-new
1958 Chevrolet. Eight passengers
packed and masked, some drifting off, heads nodding,
some perked and alert, chatting.
Our vintage automobile speeds in and out
of the chilly all-engulfing mist... At the checkpoint
we meet green masks and white coats:
we must disinfect hands and shoes
and have our temps taken. Still dark, we return
to the car and to tunneling through the mist.
To my right, a red-blue sky announces the sun
is waking, rising majestically from
a drowsy hill-lined horizon. A young man gasps *Wow!*
and captures the wondrously unique moment
on his cell. There are *pic-poems* everywhere you turn.
Golden light dances off palm fronds. He stores the sunrise,
I emulate in written expression. It´s good to know that
in the middle of all these COVID tension times
people show such sensitivity. COVID tries to travel
with us but it does not define us, it does not
dehumanize us.

Molly Joseph
(Kerala, India)

Molly Joseph had her doctorate in post-war American poetry. She retired as the head of the Department of English, St. Xavier's College, Aluva, Kerala, and served as a professor of Communicative English at FISAT, Kerala. Molly's interests lie primarily in Poetry, both Malayalam and English, that deals with contemporary issues. She writes travelogues, poems, and short stories (for children) and has published fifteen books—ten books of poems. She travels widely, attends national and international poetry festivals, and has won several accolades and awards. She writes in international journals and many international online journals and magazines. She has been awarded several times.

NEW DAWN

A new world awakens
to a new dawn…
while the gentle wind
wafts in whispering the
provenance, permutations, promises
the lake disturbed with
countless ripples, bubbles
grows calm, and the pebbles that fell on it
lie still in peace in depths.

march ahead we must,
mustering courage.

masked let us explore
the masked mysteries of life…
trees we were in distanced solitude,
but we survived the storm…

though denuded of its leaves and branches,
we entrenched our roots firm
in the living earth, our abode we overlooked,
now keeping it pristine, precious…

crossing the river of life,
in paced abandon on its ride and tide
flowing with the flow
we learnt love, kindness…
that the other is but our own
unpredictable, sensitive self

all flickering particles
floating in space!
march ahead we must
mustering courage.

THE SUN ON THE MOUNTAINS

the Sun on the mountains
tells me.
Wake up!
wake up to the glory
of life on earth…

I am benevolent
as ever.

from primordial times
I ascended and descended
over you,
roused you up
from your stupor,
You, who stress out
your petty lives
over matters frivolous

over aeons and ages
stirring growth
oxygenating all
I enthused your
environment

they know it well
those birds, chirping my arrival,
even the lone thrush hiding yet chiding
why men fail to see
the glory that surrounds
his average life.

to see another morn,
to breathe in and out

the air so fresh that flows, tickling
the blossoms that wave in the air
cuddled by the lush green
rooted firm on slopes of hilltops
celebrating life ..

I am. benevolent as ever.

wake up to the glory
of life on earth.

Neelam Saxena
(Pune, Maharashtra, India)

Neelam Saxena works as an Additional Divisional Railway Manager, Pune. She has authored five novels, one novella and six short story collections, 31 poetry collections, and 13 children's books. She is a bilingual writer, writing in English and Hindi. She holds a record with the Limca Book of Records, 2015, for being the author having the highest number of publications in a year in English and Hindi. She was rewarded with many prizes and listed in Forbes as one of the 78 most famous authors in the country in 2014.

NEW YEAR 2020

The new year blows the bugle,
The old year retreats,
I have no choice but to follow
The rhythms of nature
And I bow to the passing year,
Hug him tight,
And then bid a good-bye with a smile,
Despite knowing that I am going
To miss him like crazy!

By now, I've become quite used
To the passing of old years,
Like yellow leaves dropping from the trees,
And new leaves blooming on them as a new year.
I try to see it with detachment-
After all, every year is meant to pass…

However, the more I struggle
To let it simply vanish,
The more it keeps appearing;
Till I finally give up.
Yes, though the year may go away,
The memories and the feelings associated
Shall always remain embedded in the heart.

2020! You were particularly special!
In the chaos of Corona,
You taught me how to survive
Not only the virus,
But also contain the fear;
I must have hugged you a thousand times
When I felt lost, lonely or low;
And you were always there for me,

Embracing me with all my nervousness,
Teaching me how to be strong
And helped me build an edifice all around me
Which could block all negative energies!

Adieu 2020!
You simply cannot just pass—
You will remain in so many hearts—
Some will curse you,
Some will praise you,
But no one would ever forget you
For, you were the one who taught
The real meaning of resilience!

THAT FIRST STEP

You don't always remain confined
To your locked grey rooms,
You learn to crawl out on your weak knees,
You steady yourself, imparting them strength,
You slowly straighten yourself,
Energy comes into your being,
You take the first unsteady step,
Then you begin to stride,
Till finally you start climbing
The rungs of those long stairs
That had once seemed impossible
To even approach with your nervous being!

Nothing is permanent in this world,
Not even darkness!

Nicola Frangicne
(Forenza, Italy)

Nicola Frangione was born in Forenza (Potenza), Italy, in 1953. Performance Art and Action Poetry to participate in numerous international shows and festivals. He has been living and working in Monza since 1972 as an interdisciplinary artist, experimenting with several techniques: visual arts, audio art, sound poetry, video art, and visual poetry. He has published and produced several art books. National and international radio stations have broadcast some of his audio works. Some of his videos were released on TV, and since 2003 he has been the Art Director of "ART ACTION" International Performance Art Festival in Monza, Italy.

ACTION POETRY IN RESILIENCE

In the sense of poetics, the poet prepares, convocates, orders a
    sacrifice,
works poetic art.
In poetics, the word is not disembodied, it has not yet been
    taken from
the body.
The word acts in the poet, who exhibits his own things totally,
    through the
anguish of his own existence and the process of non-theatrical
    dramatization
The poet in the first place uses the means, purer, more repug-
    nant
and refined, that he possesses: the muscle body, the nerve body.
In the performance, or poetic act, the body is loosened from all
functionality, has no tasks to bring to term, stops making itself
    useful.
Hands grasp emptiness, close over objects full of poetic inti-
    macy.
Legs are fractured to accelerate the race inside being. Lips do not
    open,
the word dies feebly, certain of its silence.
The skinless poet in his turn skins the word. Breaking the word,
    the poet
investigates the chastity and enchantment of the trembling body.
Working thus, he divides the word from itself, he cuts its mouth.
The poet plays life, surrounding the resonant body with a silence
    that sinks
the word.
Each word hides an abyss, lives its song in the burnings of the
    poet body.
This totality of language distances the performer from himself,
    suspends
him in the utopia of communion.

284

The soul of the poet-performer is a ball made of water,
an identical, non-reading hole with a humid entrance.
His house is recovered with wind. Enlarging, it will have five
   stains on a
lightless altar and a faceless theatre of stone.

Norbert Góra
(Jastrzębia, Poland)

Norbert Góra is a 31-year-old poet and writer from Poland. He is the author of more than 100 poems which have been published in poetry anthologies in USA, UK, India, Nigeria, Kenya and Australia.

WE ROSE FROM THE ASHES

Wreckage everywhere,
as far the eye can see,
though it wasn't
a conflagration of the war.
We have lost our joy,
but the faith hasn't been eradicated,
we rose from the ashes
like a phoenix.
We will build a new world here,
removing our old bloody sins,
to rise above pride,
division and selfishness,
to create a better future
under the umbrella of equality,
unity will shine like the sun.
One day we will mention
a chapter of pandemic
in the book of life,
then everything
will be clear,
it was a sign
for mental changes.

Old Captain of Three Gorges
(Baotou City, Inner Mongolia, Mongolia)

Xu Jiangang, A pseudonym, Old Captain Three Gorges, male, Baotou City, Inner Mongolia. Professor of British and American Literature, Three Gorges University, Master tutor, Ministry of Education doctoral thesis evaluation expert. 2004, Visiting Scholar, University of Griffith, Australia. 2008, Exchange Professor, University of Memphis, USA. He is currently a professor at the International College of Wenzhou Business School. April 1983, first published *Poetry*. He has published more than 100 literary and academic papers in magazines at all levels

ON THE EARTH, ON THE WAY

Talking about who I am
Tears overflowed from the left eye
My name was changed three times
From then on, the body was surrounded by walls
I gave myself a pseudonym:
Old Captain
It's like a Mongolian's horse-head string without lyrics
No beginning, no ending

And talking about where do I belong
I think of the seeds of dandelion
Taking off from the Sillingler prairie
Watching over the wheat fields in the Jianghan plain
Not down follow the flow of the Hanjiang River
But striking against the waves of the Three Gorges of the
    Yangtze River

An old man of his late year
Wearing already a bloody head
The body and mind are torn into pieces
A ragged sack alike
Deep in his left ventricle
But always hide the pride of the old horse

Finally, talking about where am I going
Suddenly a burst of melancholy in the bottom of my heart
    growing crazy
Looking at the Rhone thousands of miles away
Force himself to measure with his feet the last distance

Peggy Morrison
(San Francisco, California, USA)

Peggy Morrison is a California poet who lives and works in the San Francisco Bay Area. She has read poetry in English and Spanish in the US, Mexico and Cuba, and published in journals and anthologies. She has published one book of poetry: *Mom Says* (2020). Peggy is a mom and she is a bilingual teacher committed to working for social justice. She loves reading, teaching, gardening, music, and backpacking.

SIP DAY 356,
THIS MORNING IN THE GARDEN

There is a juvenile pear tree suddenly
full of delicate
white flowers trembling
thread-like pistils

a translucent orange-brown
salamander blending in with the dirt
so still that we think it might
be dead

then it moves like a ripple
the microscopic gripping fingers
of its front hand
its transparent eyes still

an army of viola seedlings are
sprouting all around the mother plants
in the black soil.

Dan harvests the kale before it goes to seed.
Vanya gathers arugula from the dense feathered patch.
I sauté broccoli for lunch.

THE RIVERBED GAZING UP AT THE STARS

Each star pulling a thread of light from sky to earth
The sky breath breathed by lungs rising and falling, rising and
falling
stomata and alveoli inhale and exhale in communion
bathe in shared air

The shared air holding living cells of memory
The memories held in common by ancient redwood
and slim seedling beneath
The slim seedling feels water coursing through its veins
The same veins of our human history, our many grandmothers
Our many grandmothers speaking their many voices
Their voices ring in our ears
sing in our many dreams
swirl in our one dream
an illusive moment of tenderness
forest quiet
gazing eye

The child gazing up into the mother's face
The mother's milk nourishing the child
The child's love pulling a thread of history from the womb
through ocean depths
deep as time

Peter Londi Lwal
(Kisumu, Nyanza, Kenya)

Peter Londi Lwal pursued higher education at the Great Lakes University of Kisumu and graduated with a Bachelor of Science Degree in Community Health and Development Honors. Peter has worked for nonprofit charitable organizations serving vulnerable children, youth, and caregivers. Currently, he does consultancy services and is particularly passionate about poetry, child rights, peace and conflict resolution, and community development. In 2020, his poem "Amazing Order" was published in an anthology of poems, *Soaring above the Pandemic: Poetic Echoes from East Africa*.

A GATE CRASHER

Just a simple fine cough
At the Vic. Beach in the gulf
Triggers an incessant sneeze
That interrupts a retreat in the breeze

Causing a shift in the schedule
To swift Adam in a shuttle
As taking in oxygen is a rare gift
Heart beats pound in gilt
Exposing ingratitude lifestyle
For nothing is for granted on the tile.

In search for a common commodity
People pensively gape in the community
Many heads are tossed into the soil
White and black no longer toil
Tall and short are the same
Sceptre and silver are in shame
Strong and weak are alike
As wise and foolish are in lack

The mystery of the twenty first century
That narrows the road to the sanctuary
Shaking the strong painfully
To stop pointing at the cross playfully
But put priestly pyramids in place
To regain the glory of the highest palace
And upholds her salty utility
For reaching dark hearts in totality

The globe is at sea
Nations' goldmines cease
Institutions are at stake
As everyone is stuck
Prompting many to hang
Bowing to hunger pang

Where are the learned lords?
To declare death sentences to corona loads
The Almighty is involved
With a fatherly rod
To bring a change
By removing the strange
Availing a valuable viral vaccine
That begins brightening socio-economic scene

TRANQUILITY

Stop talking at each other
It generates volcanoes between you and another
Like to a puppy lively
Talk with people lovely

Stormy waves, human imperfection
Everyone, selfish perception
The pursuit of throne and silver
That pollutes societal savor

We ought to listen in our hearts
And interact in our acts
Visiting neighbors to forestall hurts
And assist kinsmen to decently wear hats.

Eschew volcanic violence
Look at a coin with double love-lens
Exploring our diversity
And appreciate humanity

As tacticians of peace
We facilitate wars to cease
And allow time to reconstruct trust
As scary scars in society's past rust

Never shall we be the same
Yet this should not be for blame
I must see your unique energy
And create a super synergy

Pravat Kumar Padhy
(Bhubaneswar, Odisha, India)

Susheel Kumar Sharma (b. 1962) has been serving the University of Allahabad, Prayagraj (India), as a Professor of English since 2003. He has published several books, research papers, interviews, and book reviews and is a creative writer too. Some of his poems have been internationally published and translated into other languages. Susheel Kumar Sharma was conferred the 'AESI Lifetime Achievement Award 2020' of the Association for English Studies of India.

A New Dawn
the sun
cleanses clouds of darkness
subtle dream
I stare at the distant horizon
where morning sky kisses the sea

window filters
the layers of freshness
how wonderfully
like a tender money plant
we rush ahead chasing brightness

an old man
in the garden path
caresses lilacs
enthralling at every step
as winter gives way to spring

kids swing and play
like flowers in the garden
their smiles
rejuvenate once again
reaching beyond the fence

old couple
with wrinkled smiles
spreads ripples of happiness
birds with the little ones
gratify everyone the joy of living

from dawn to dusk
life becomes so amusing
the enduring muse
as if reaches the stars
dancing under the moonlit sky

Preety Sengupta
(Ahmedabad, India / New York, USA)

Preety Sengupta is from India, and has been living in New York for many years. She writes Poetry, essays and short stories in both English and Gujarati, her mother-tongue. She is also a novelist, and translates from other languages as well. Her books have received many prizes and Awards. Her work is included in several anthologies in India and in USA.

INCHING OUT OF THE TUNNEL

There used to be a train that moved constantly.
Not so new, but it was shiny and comfortable.
A local train, it moved slowly,
Making stops every so often, with passengers
          getting on and off.
I liked it that way. The slow-going.
The hustle and bustle of stops,
The interesting configurations of platforms.
And oh, all those countless different names
—they fascinated constantly.
I could conjure up images of places afar, unseen.

It used to be a lovely journey
—lovely, easy, safe.
Oh yes, safe, surely.

That train has been stuck in a mysterious tunnel,
For the length of time that is immeasurable.
The opening of the tunnel can be guessed,
          not seen yet.

Let the train inch forward
—to the living, breathing possibilities.
Azure skies are stretched out there,
And the meadows of newly-blossomed flowers.
Let's have patience - a little longer,
For Smiles to spill off many lips,
For Joy to dance in many eyes,
For Hope to fill up many hearts
Again, and forever, from now on.

Purnima Kulkarni
(Pune, India)

Purnima Kulkarni is a research scholar, motivational speaker, soft skills trainer, poetess, content writer, creative writer and a professor of English at UG and PG level. She is Co-Editor of an International Journal called Literary Horizon. She completed her Doctorate n English from SPPU, Pune, and has established an institute of her own called Dr. Purnima Kulkarni's Discourses: A Centre for English Language, Literature and Culture.

FEAR NOT

Sometimes we're filled with despondency, dread and doom,
Our heart turns into a bleak, dark and empty room,
Our head is swamped with blackened gloom,
And happy songs get out of tune!

At times, we're woeful, weary and battle-sore,
And we think we can't take it anymore,
Panic attacks come to the fore,
And strike us hard, down, on the floor!

We feel scared when we're almost dying,
But we must trust Krishna, the LORD, see I'm not lying,
God can turn woes, tribulations and sighing,
Into joy and bliss, where angels are curveting flying!

We can spot the Lord on His divine throne,
Where He resides in his Heaven's Home,
If we offer our sincere obeisance to Him on our own,
And allow prayers flow in the blood of our veins, nay in the very
    bones!

Sometimes happiness sings a dirge and sounds our death knell,
We suffer, sigh, rot and groan when unwell,
We will never ever be punished in Hell,
As Krishna will rescue us and exclaim, All is well!

He will gift us all, a brand - new spiritual dress,
And an eternal body of righteousness,
Because we are honoured, privileged and thoroughly blessed,
So never give up, fume, fret or stress!

For when we mortal humans take our final breath,
Kissed by the angel we all call "death",

We'll see Lord Krishna's light and arms outstretched,
No longer would we be dejected, sad, lost, or bereft!

Marvellous wonders will no longer wait,
As we produce our Karmic balance sheets at the Heaven's gate,
Where no tears fall and no hearts break,
Unprecedented joy and peace we'll taste!

So, do not fear the Reaper's scythe,
For Krishna will be right by our side,
Indomitable power will help us rise,
To Glory's heights, where angels glide!

ENDURANCE

You grumble, complain, crib and feel it's only you,
And think that no one struggles the way you do,
But Almighty Lord reminds you that there are many more,
Who battle demons that obstruct each day's chore!

All around the world there are others too,
Who share the same trial's painful view,
Turbulent times are nothing new,
Excruciating pain does envelope a few!

Learn to be resilient when times are tough,
And troubled seas are harsh and rough,
Focus on Krishna the Lord, in the storm—
His peace and love will keep you warm!

Krishna will make sure that you do not drown,
Though trying times drag you down,
He's always there, so never frown,
He'll keep you enveloped with His cloak and gown!

When vicissitudes of life harshly grate,
And you're bent so low with their enormous weight,
Krishna will share the load and ease your pain,
Befriend Him as it shall never be in vain!

Sometimes, your heart may weep and ache,
The Lord will support you, so you'll never break,
His love will sustain through the gloomy shadows long,
For when you're weak and fragile, His grace is strong!

NEVER GIVE UP

Life is a vast ocean that's deep, far and wide,
You just don't know what is waiting within its high tide,
Some days it's a pleasure to just bob-along,
With small lapping ripples and a heart full of song!

Sometimes the water is cantankerous and violently rages,
Learning to swim against the current may take ages,
Are there any monsters lurking? Do you dread looking down?
Never give up your fortitude as they'd ensure that you drown!

It's an uphill task to focus when waves roar and chase,
That buffet you off-course and splash on your face,
Sometimes you hear sirens who tempt you to veer,
Away from your purpose as they reverberate in your ear!

For your course should forever be full-steam-ahead,
Orcas and Giant Whales would be your Chaperons instead,
Krishna the Lord will always show you the way,
Have unfathomable faith and you'll never go astray!

So, listen to His voice & just keep on accelerating,
He'll be right there with you, through gales and tempests
    exasperating,
He'll keep your head upright when legs start to cramp,
And when it gets dark, His love shall be your lamp!

Jellyfish will sting and electric eels will shock,
His Hope and Grace will draw you to His fortress and rock,
Where you will find eternal joy, peace and rest,
The sight of Krishna's face will leave you breathless and blessed!

Pushmaotee Subrun
(Mauritius)

Pushmaotee Subrun, born in Mauritius, studied in Delhi University, worked in Zimbabwe and Mauritius, was later a member of the Council of the University of Mauritius and is currently an editor in the Ministry of Arts and Culture. Her poems have featured in prestigious online magazines and anthologies. *Amaravati Poetic Prism* 2018 and 2019, *Destiny Poets*, selected as Poet and critic of ICOP Awards 2019, inner child press international anthology-Poets for Humanity, World Healing and in World Peace International Poetry Symposium, April 2020.

LET US SEEK FOR THE GUIDING LIGHT

Hope and triumph, we wish we had,
The alarm, the fear and the horror is still bad.
When millions of precious lives have been lost
And we have been tempest tossed,
For better times we are waiting hopefully,
With vaccinations the death toll will go down surely.
What is left is to arm ourselves bravely,
Yes, face the music of life stoically.

Let us motivate ourselves to embrace a simple world, peaceful,
Where everything is beautiful,
Where there is love, peace, fraternity,
Forbidding harassment, lessening enmity,
Mitigating violence to the vulnerable,
Lessening rape, brutal killing and squabble,
Discouraging addiction, racism, secularization,
Domestic violence, divorce and separation.

We need to preach humanity, for the downtrodden engage,
Respect and consideration for people, the Lord's image.
Yes, let us all inculcate through the poets' healing verses,
Melting prejudices, encouraging to accept differences,
To live and let live, to encourage justice,
To cast away ego and pride to the wind,
Where nothing will be lost but instead bind.

In a bid to seek for unity, let us seek for the guiding light,
In this dark maze of life, turn sufferings to beacons of light.
Thus, dispiriting the steps of betrayal becomes a must,
Ultimately rebuilding empathy, love and trust,
Before we human beings return to dust.
Indeed, in our confinement, let us nourish our souls
And hope that the Lord's mercy will duly shine on us all.

RESILIENCE AND HOPE

Hope is what has always sustained humanity,
Why not hope for a better day in unanimity?
When our natural world has revived,
The smog over Los Angeles has cleared,
The snow-capped Himalayas have cleared its mists,
The earth's upper crust has calmed according to seismologists.
All wonderful reminders that nothing lasts forever,
Undoubtedly, the pandemic will not last forever.
The world is threatened with the domino effect ominously,
Bankruptcies, unemployment and Chinese Whispers,
    portentously.
But what we need is dose of optimism imminently.
.

We might not win immediately,
But surely, we shall win ultimately.
Airports are not functioning normally
Due to our health being a priority.
Retailers, casino workers, restaurants, universities,
Factories and all sectors will soon be like busy bees.
The media is spreading news of recession
Or a collapse of our society with depression,
And food shortages or other ticking time bombs.
Discouraging news to lead us earlier to our tombs!
Best is to boost our moral strength with encouraging
    aplomb!

Replenishing the self is more than vital,
Nurturing our inner world for better survival,
What with continuous challenges, revitalizing our batteries,
It's crucial to reconnect with those elevating galaxies,
And do something we enjoy deeply, for once,
Like spending quality time in confinement with loved ones,
In vitalizing, refreshing nature walking and breathing,

With ourselves and our environment reconnecting,
For ideally healing, far from morbid thoughts engaging.
With new life in us, we shall definitely get rid of stress
And positive qualities harness.

So, let us steel ourselves mentally, physically,
And spiritually to bounce enthusiastically.
With the key coping mechanism
Of using valuable time to bring new enthusiasm,
Opening the mind to beneficial alternatives
Such as exercising, reading, painting or other derivatives,
Like poetry writing, watching inspiring or comic films or clips,
Going on YouTube for motivational trips,
Calling friends, uplifting their morale, trying new recipes,
Or engaging in sensational potted plants to promote
   cheerfulness.
For after all, being productive will bring about wellness.

Moreover, with unwavering faith, instil,
The air with fervent thanks and good vibes fill,
For bestowed blessings by the Almighty's Will.
Let hope, prayer and faith illuminate and fulfil,
As they strengthen realism that we can prevail.
Let's confront the brutal facts, and opportunities avail,
Incessantly imploring the Heavens for mercy on us to prevail.
Nothing will our determination mar,
If we be in hope as fixed as the Northern Star.
Come thunder, lightning or rain,
However, blighted our lot, our stars will shine again!

Ranko Pavlović
(Banja Luka, Bosnian and Herzegovina)

Ranko Pavlović (1943) is a writer, poet, essayist, literary critic, and playwright. He writes for children and adults. He has published twenty collections of poems, seven novels, two collections of essays, a book of literary criticism, and ten radio dramas for adults. Also, 18 collections of short stories for children, six of poems for the youngest, two novels for young people, ten plays for theaters for children, and about twenty radio plays for children. His poems and short stories have been translated into different languages. He has received almost all significant literary awards in Serbia and Bosnia and Herzegovina and was nominated for the prestigious world award for children's literature 'Astrid Lindgren.'

THE SPIRIT OF SHAKESPEARE BETWEEN US

Translated by Danijela Trajković

Who plays you any more today in the theatre,
my Shakespeare? They play with you, chop you,
have you naked, put a mobile phone
in Julia's hands, Romeo is sent
on formula 1 racings. What can I tell you?
They feed their fate by damaging your
texts. It's like they say, they're directors
of New Age, they don't care, can do
with the old English what they want.
They can, whenever wish, set Hamlet
for the board president of the world's largest
corporations for the production of preservatives,
and the spirit of his father lay in a thermos bottle
and have the drink with cold coke,
at the tennis tournament, that's now in fashion,
as in your time were knights' tournaments.
Like the creators of the new world order,
who walk the world as if it was only theirs,
the same way new directors tailor your drama.
But, Shakespeare, grab your pen again
(when the spirit of Hamlet's father still walks
the world, you can also), so write
something new, let's say about global
warming up and humiliating relationship
according to the gay population, though
the texts will be looked at and thrown
under the table as far as possible from the scene
by the theatre directors, who will continue on their own.
But, don't worry, your time is coming.

HUNTING

Translated by Svetlana Pavlovic

We hunted grasshoppers and butterflies,
Just to have enough play in the meadow…

…then we hunted rabbits and roebucks,
Just to gorge ourselves and to survive,

Then we hunted foxes and wolves,
to stop them hunting our rabbits and roebucks,

then we hunted other hunters,
to stop them hunting our quarry…

…so we started to hunt ourselves,
for he who once starts hunting— never stops.

Raúl Henao
(Medellín, Colombia)

Raúl Henao (Cali, Colombia, 1944). He has lived in Venezuela, México, and the United States. He has books released and is in important Ibero American and world anthologies published. His poetic work has been partially translated into English, French, German, Portuguese, Rumanian, and Swedish.

HAIKU

A police check.
Did I forget to pay
at the entrance to paradise?

OBLIVION

Translated by Cindy Schuster

Encircles the dispossessed the forsaken
Oblivion walks its dead
Unburied amid the fog
Pierces the deaf man the street he crosses
His blood leaps, signaling him
In the mirror of morning.
And there's not a tree in sight
Where you could put a nest of birds
Not a single cloud to encamp the Sun.

Oblivion walks its unburied dead
In encircles the dispossessed the forsaken.
The deaf man crosses the street.
Amid the fog the birds encamp
For there is no sun where you could place a cloud
No tree to erase
The bloodstorm of dawn.

Ravindra Pratap Singh (R.P.Singh)
(Uttar Pradesh, India)

R P Singh (Ravindra Pratap Singh) is a Professor of English at the Department of English and Modern European Languages, University of Lucknow. He is an award-winning playwright, poet, essayist, and academician. A frequently anthologized poet in more than 20 prestigious anthologies and has published more than 300 poems and popular articles in newspapers and magazines. He has received 16 awards for his creative writing, innovations in teaching, and commendable contribution to Higher Education.

THE ETERNAL SUSTENANCE

Come thoughts again
splendid and shaped,
Images dwindle
and the reflections to twitch.

Poetry comes again to keep,
come, you, again
in retrospection so deep.

Poetry comes when moves do fail
and feelings moan to go,
poetry, glides, and moves across.

Verses come as a chum on a loss,
yes, when threshold is tolled
and the moves stalked.

Happy or sad
something fathomed, or a fad,
the world comes
within the thought.
So flux a time
expressions' authentic sound,
and the words move on.
Words bring love
and peace they build,
the eternal sustenance.

The parched-up grass
and the dried-up land
  squirms for the nectar drops,
  the loving nectar comes,
  will was strong.

Yearning for a new sprout
yearning for the soot to smile
yearning for the leaves lush green.

The minuses become a plus,
and the dawn again.
The phase was weird
smitten to self a dingy shell.
The phase is gone,
now benevolent spell.
Will makes will,
And efforts' cordons are seen
  towards a brighter self.

Ronny Someck
(Tel Aviv, Israel)

Ronny Someck was born in Baghdad in 1951 and came to Israel as a young child. He has published 13 volumes of poetry, the last one being *So Much God.* He also has two books for children published that have been translated into 43 languages. Selections of his poems have appeared in a good number of translations. He is a recipient of several artistic awards

.

A POEM OF BLISS

We are placed on a wedding cake
like the two dolls, bride and groom.
when the knife strikes
We'll try to stay on the same slice.

Richard Marvin Tiberius (Tai) Grove
(Brighton, Ontario, Canada)

Richard Marvin Grove, otherwise known to friends as Tai, divides his time between Toronto and Brighton. He is a poet, prose writer, publisher, photographer, painter, graphic designer, the Poet Laureate of Brighton, and the founding president of the CCLA—Canada Cuba Literary Alliance. He has almost 20 titles to his name, and his images have been used in many books and on the cover of nearly 75 books. He has had over 100 poems and essays published in periodicals around the world, as well as having been published in over 50 anthologies. His art and photographs are in over 30 corporate collections across Canada. He graduated from Ontario College of Art in 1984. and with honors from Humber College Arts Admin.

THE LAST SUNSET

January 01, 2021

Dear Family and Friends:
I went for a last walk
to our Presqu'ile Point Lighthouse
with Kim and dear friends
on the last evening of 2020.
The calm and tranquil time
of love and camaraderie
was greeted with a stunning sunset.
If we had headed to that
swell-swept grey-pebbled beach
a few minutes earlier, or later,
we might have missed the splendor.

That last sunset of 2020 was stupendous,
existing in a fearless, covid-free realm
of perfection. I imagined sharing
that moment with thousands,
maybe millions of equally stunned
blue-marble dwellers, all in awe with me.
I had to contemplate,
is there anything new under the sun,
except for our growing willingness
to plunge deeper with our faith
into a new pool of hope?

The restrictions imposed on us in 2020,
have of course, severely limited
our physical opportunities
but as we closed out our walk,
turning towards home, I thought
that there will be more togetherness
in the days to come, more

reasons to be grateful
for our faith in our fulfilled expectations.
As special as it was
on an ethereal, experiential level
to see that last sunset of 2020
it will not be the last. The next sunset,
the fifth, the hundredth from now,
will be as cherished as this last of 2020.

The sun, the clouds, the waves,
the redness, the orange
will never be repeated in exactly this way
but now that we have slipped into 2021
we are offered
a growing faith and trust in love
that our every need will be met
and smooth the way
to our expressions of a joy-filled life.

Rie Sheridan Rose
(Austin, Texas, USA)

Rie Sheridan Rose multitasks. A lot. Her poetry appears in numerous venues, including Speculative Poets of Texas, Vol. 1; Texas Poetry Calendar; and Illumen to name a few. She has authored six poetry chapbooks, twelve novels, and lyrics for dozens of songs.

MELTING THE ICE

The world has been encased in ice,
households frozen in stasis.
People locked inside their homes,
watching news of deadly avalanches of cases.

The ice grew to icebergs
forcing isolation or dreadful consequences.
Edges rubbed to brittle sharpness
as we lost all sense of time and place.

But now, the spring is coming.
The ice begins to weep as the sun rises.
The sharp prick of a bee sting vaccine,
and the flower of hope raises its head.

As the world warms to a new season,
it seems the ice of quarantine is falling away.
It isn't gone, but it is going…
and the ice is melting from our hearts.

We shall hug again in time,
visit people and places that we have missed.
The ice will yield to science if we let it.
And the sun will shine again on Earth.

Runa Pathak Uppal
(New Delhi, India)

Runa Pathak Uppal is a seasoned Corporate Social Responsibility Professional with a demonstrated history of working in the pharmaceuticals industry. She plays a crucial role in the effective implementation of CSR projects of Jubilant Bhartia Group. Runa is the recipient of several awards like the Value-able Employee Award, Spot On Awards for outstanding performance, and Best Team Award (CSR Team). Runa is fond of writing and has written over 200 poems and blogs in Hindi and English. Her poems and articles get published regularly in leading newspapers in India. She is an alumnus of Banaras Hindu University. Her pen name is Runa Lakhnavi.

THE DISASTER

It's time for unveiling the stage again
Hope you and me always remember
the pain…
the continuous pain!
The isolation in homes,
the empty streets,
the fear of only loss and no gain!

The nature was at its profusion,
mistakes tracked
and lessons learned!
from brink of trouble for the human race,
with money, the happiness can't be earned!

The evergreen shadows
and the souls we lost
during the disaster at own cost
engraving these learning for the new bloom
the love, affection and care
are treasured for whom?

BEGINNING OF AN ERA

Covid tried us all and tried with lockdown
It hit us hard and brought us down
The agony and pain
Will it hit us hard once again?

Hoping to see the smiling faces
And the memories with traces
Was it an end of game
Or beginning of an era with new name

Sahaj Sabharwal
(Jammu city, J&K, India)

Sahaj Sabharwal lives in Jammu city, Kashmir, India. His date of birth is 17th March, 2002. He has received many awards in poetry writing including the 'India Star Proud Award' for his work. He has published one poetry book.

MOONLIGHT'S ADDICTION

It's dark night,
Still you are bright.
It's night, to sleep right?
Still our eyelids fight
To be closed tight
But your beauty forces them to remain polite,
To have an uninterrupted sight.
You are creamish white,
Making dark sky and earth, look bright.
My paining neck complaining that you are upright.
Despite all you are quite quiet.
Hidden warrior as complimentary heart for many broken hearts,
    numbered as infinite.
Especially for you, today I write.
After the sun's departure, I shall wait for your invite,
To listen to my submitted rhyming poem that you will recite.
But still my eyelids will try again to sleep tonight.
Please make our dissent night a decent good night.

Sally Quon
(Kelowna, British Columbia, Canada)

Sally Quon is a back-country blogger, dirt-road diva, and teller of tales. Choosing to express herself through poetry, photography, and creative non-fiction, Sally has been published in all three. In 2020, she was a finalist in the Vallum Chapbook Award and The Muriel's Journey Poetry Prize. Her work has appeared in numerous anthologies. Sally is an associate member of the League of Canadian Poets. Her bucket list is entirely about bears.

CASCADE

emerging from a condo chrysalis
to a cabin in the woods
where water
tumbles, froths
wispy-white and olive brown
raucous laughter
crushing restless mind

mourning cloaks chase each other and the breeze
cottonwood fluff floating

sunlight moves over pools
unwrapping each new facet like a gift
and even the shadows are filled with color

american dippers fly the face of the falls
perch on boulders, bob, and dive

all around the water flows

paths, once divergent
coalesce into one

a first step
tentative, hopeful

Sangram Jena
(Bhubaneswar, Odisha, India)

Sangram Jena has published three volumes of poetry in English and five collections of poems in Odia. His poems have been published in India and abroad in several prestigious journals. His poems have been included in several anthologies published in India and abroad. He has translated many ancient and medieval Odia Poets into English and Classics of English Literature into Odia. He has received Sahitya Academi Award (National Academy of Letters, India). He edits Marg Asia, a Literary Journal in English published by the Centre for Asian Studies, Bhubaneswar, Odisha, India.

SACRED HOUR

I live at a place
where my ancestors'
memories are buried.

An uncanny belief
that all will not be the same
hunts me now and then.

I slowly forget those lonely moments
when the shadows of the dead
knocked at my doors
in the dark of the night
urging me to allow them
to enter the home where
they lived a few days ago.
The night lies still
and quietly under my skin
through lingering pain and grief.

As the night ripens
I feel a scented wind
coming through my half-open door
and moonlight thrashing my window panes,
the chirping of an unknown bird
is heard in the fading darkness
as a pure generosity of love.

I wonder if I am not
looking for something
I used to have some time back,
something stolen from me
and now far beyond my reach
like lost pages of memories and meditations.

I feel someone comes in and tells me to shout:
'Look the morning is not far away'…

EVERYTHING WILL HAPPEN AGAIN

There are days and days
anything can happen any day.

In the autumn the withered tree
stretches its frail hands towards the horizon,
standing sad and silent.
In the spring you find
nests hanging from its lush bonny branches.
Seasons and climate change
but the quiet stillness returns at the end.

Waves in the sea rise and fall,
pushed away from the shore.
They come back a moment after,
like unsuspected breathings.

Dreams preserve those forgotten faces,
each time the heart talks about something past,
they come out like stars in a dark night.

The body remembers
each small thing lost
returning your doubts and fears.
The longings return through rain's unnoticed visits
choosing its own time and place.

We always keep accounts of deaths and births
to understand the clarity of things,
what we find everyday
is a blind return to history and memory.

347

After a while
Life is back to its own place.

Setaluri Padmavathi
(Hyderabad, India)

Setaluri Padmavathi, a postgraduate in English Literature with a B.Ed., has over three decades of experience in the field of education.
She held various positions like the Head of the Department of English, Academic Coordinator, Principal, and Teacher during her professional career. Writing has always been her passion; she translates it into poems of different genres, short stories, and articles on various themes and topics.

PEACE AND TRIUMPH

The doors of freedom shut in a way, long ago
The progressive world lost its growth and glow
Poverty and unemployment raised on the earth
For a while, the entire world forgot to display mirth!

The contagious virus spread rapidly everywhere
People stopped moving on the busy thoroughfare
Lifestyle altered for the sake of the state's health
Growth of all interrupted, including commonwealth!

Fear of death and worry of disease troubled all
But the scientists joined their hands for its fall
Vaccine was discovered for people's protection
All nations were ready to go for an injection!

Gloomy days make the countries stressful
Hope is the only way to become successful
Strengthen your mind, fear not for the state
I opine and trust, there is a future opening gate!

You're not isolated anymore like before
Peaceful days and triumph are in store
Online education and tasks became life
Let's together find the solution for strife!

Covid warriors strive very hard to serve
Awareness programs are done to observe
Patience might help us have days, bright
Resilience makes our troubled hearts light!

HOPE

These saddened days may turn into good days soon
The dark period would pass like a passing cloud
Let's hope for a better morrow, with positive thoughts
We'd fly high like free winged and chirping birds!

We waged the dreadful wars and had seen great loss
We overcame Spanish flew, cyclones, and storms
We're fingers crossed for a new medical discovery
Let's pray for the global health, peace and happiness!

Fear not like a trembling water bird, you're brave!
Worry not for changing times, they bring solace too,
Don't be panic for today, you'd see a better morrow
Come on! Cheer up! The shadowy world would see glow!

You would join your hands with the moving humanity
You'll be the part and parcel of every action of society
You would also cherish the fruitful life and happy days
These tough times will pass like the moving clouds!

All barren lands would certainly turn into farmlands
All enthusiastic men would busily work in firms
All means of transport will soon open new avenues
Let's use the earthly possessions to develop ourselves!

Let's go hand in hand to be more productive than before
Let's build our nation in each and every nook and corner
We, as capable human beings, see the bright side of life
and eliminate the darkness from this beautiful world!

Shakes Khan
(Nanjing, China)

Shakes Khan, a distinguished Chinese poet, writer, and critic, was born in the 1960s in Southern Anhui Province, now living in Nanjing. He served as a journalist, editor-in-chief, adjunct professor, visiting scholar of Peking University, and counselor for government, educational and art, and literary organizations, and now he is engaged in research, association of art, and literature, and on the editorial board of the Chinese Makers of Art & Literature. With numerous works of prose, poetry, and criticism that appeared in periodicals and anthologies, and over ten books published, he has won more than ten national awards for literature and criticism.

IN THE DEAD SILENCE

Translated by Bai Shui

The candlelight flickered, went out by the wind
A veil of fog grows, avoiding eye sockets
Flowing blood hits the sparks

Rivers and streams frozen with full of ice
it eliminates their cracks
Covered the proliferation of caves and caverns

Like a flourishing period
swirling, flickering, twisting seasons
full of pain everywhere, affecting inner and outer lives

Withstood a great crisis this year
a flock of birds flying over two big falls of snow
humankind will be shocked by the history
we are hoping, expecting, believing…

Shruti Goswami
(Haldia, West Bengal, India)

Shruti Goswami is an Architect and Urban Planner from West Bengal and has numerous English poems published in several national and international anthologies and poetry websites and Bengali stories published in magazines and a leading Bengali daily. Some of her translation works also appear regularly in Navotthan, a publication of Hindusthan Samachar. She also wrote regularly for banglalive.com. Her poems have also been recited in online poetry shows in Canada.

She has published three poetry books, acted in a short film, composed poems for two Bengali short movies, and translated Bengali short film scripts into English.

WHEN THE GLOOM TIDES

The winds break the stillness of the day,
Birds chirp and the flowers
Blooming, come out of hiding
Rains and a few people get wet, drenched
Perhaps, the gloom is tiding
Away,
Come out, of desolation
Desperation for human touch and feel
Come out, then, of isolation
Let your lonely souls heal
Heave a sigh of relief
The year, nemesis for uncountable souls
That departed too early
We could only weep
Come out, then, to wish and to hope,
Tomorrow is always another day
Come out, connect, see each other
Maskless, but not homeless
Not jobless, not anymore
Come out, then, of isolation
Hear the whole world call.

Sourav Sarkar
(Cooch Behar, West Bengal, India)

Sourav Sarkar was born in Cooch Behar district, West Bengal, India. He went to Jenkins School, Cooch Behar, for higher secondary education. He graduated in English Literature from University B.T & Evening College. He did his postgraduate in English Literature from St. Joseph's college Darjeeling. His poems are published in England, India, Bangladesh, America, Canada, and Trinidad and Tobago.

ROAD THAT LEFT BEHIND

My heart says something
My words saying
Road that left behind me
Is a way to see
My days on hills
Journey much of thrills
Old cathedral stands quite
The fog comes over that place
Chilly air I can feel in my face
Good angels in white takes a plight
School boys in maroon blazers
What a lovely sight !
I stand thereby
Waiting for more to see
The beauty that makes thee
Wild flowers laughing as they know me
Since the time they born
I wish to get up in the morning
And watching them reborn
I see a placard written "God is here"
I take off my hat and asked "where?"
Then I come near by a tomb
A little wet and gloom
An old woman with red rose
Step in with some vows
I mourn with her
Pray for few minutes
As nobody stand there
I come back on road
That I left behind
And move my legs forward
Something more to find.

628 MAGAZINE ROAD

Six, two, eight are even
Straight road seems plain
Green lawns never refrain
Dogs are kept in chain
Paperboy rushes in the morning
He does live in small earning
Days of holy are evergreen
Everyone is there to share each other's pain
Hot summer dust and wintry dew
Heavy rains and paper boats
Drawn upon roads
It's name magazine
Still it does not serve
It's a road that knows how to love.

Sudeep Sen
(New Delhi, India)

Sudeep Sen has prize-winning books published and influential anthologies. His works have been translated into over 25 languages, appeared in international magazines, and broadcast on Radio stations. He is the editorial director of AARK ARTS and the editor of Atlas. Sen is the first Asian honored to deliver the Derek Walcott Lecture and read at the Nobel Laureate Festival. The Government of India awarded him for "outstanding persons in the field of culture/literature" the senior fellowship.

NINE PINS: ANOTHER OBITUARY

One by one they are dropping dead
at more than a heartbeat's rate.
I've lost nine friends in less than a week—
Mangalesh, Mahmood, Asif, Astad,
Sunil, Vikram, friends' parents/spouses…
the named and the nameless—
italicized epitaphs in multilingual script—
so many that mere counting
is like asthmatic labored wheezing—
yet another chapter of added grief.
It isn't a game of nine pins anymore—
but living souls pinned to the gallows
prematurely. Covid's curse—R.I.P.

Sue Zhu
(New Zealand)

Sue Zhu, is a New Zealand Chnese poet, artist and international cultural exchange organizer, Vice President of the New Zealand Poetry and Arts Association, Honorary Director of the US-China Culture & Art Centre, NZ representative of Italy Immagine/Poesia, Vice President of Singapore International Poetry & Art Festival, winner of over 30 international literary awards (including China). She has been invited to attend many major poetry festivals, such as the 32nd Medellin Poetry Festival, she was nominated for the Pushcart Prize in 2020 and 2021, and for the Nobel Prize in Literature in 2021, at same year she was interviewed by USA "Publishers Weekly"

Waiting for the Full Bloom

Translated by Wen Xinjiao

Sleepless thought is still awake in the deep night
Like a firefly carrying a lamp
Flying different routes to decipher
Light smiles at night

Listen to the trickling sound of water
It glides over the slope and slowly goes down along grooves
And finally merges with the sea
To make a salty cruising dreamland for fishes and seaweeds

Faded pajamas of flowers are loose and baggy
Songs of insects are kept in the past
Some love and kindness wrap around the hibernation bed
In the soft and even breathing, soothing the cold night

Right now, if one can walk through deep jungles
Cross the less traveled mountain trails
Pass through the light rain under the street light
Connect the rainbow dreams one after another

Are they all waiting
For the arrival of the full bloom

Susheel Kumar Sharma
(Allahabad Prayagraj, UP, India)

Susheel Kumar Sharma (b. 1962) has been serving the University of Allahabad, Prayagraj (India), as a Professor of English since 2003. He has published several books, research papers, interviews, and book reviews and is a creative writer too. Some of his poems have been internationally published and translated into other languages. Susheel Kumar Sharma was conferred the 'AESI Lifetime Achievement Award 2020' of the Association for English Studies of India.

THE FROG

The frog in the
Well enjoyed his life
Running and jumping
Eating moths and drinking water
While hiding under the moss
Till one day it by chance
It was pulled out
In a bucket
Attached to a Rehat
An ancient water wheel
Used by my grand parents
To water their thirsty barren fields.
The shining stars were just not visible
The frog had been blinded by the bright sun.
It jumped frantically to a scorching place
Burning its bum and limbs.
I just guess and guess
Who does it blame for its misery?
Now I understand
A frog can also make an allegory.

THE ROAD

In a yellow wood one road diverged into
Two; and happily one cannot travel both
And be a lonely traveler; long I stood
And looked for the one who could
Be one and still tread on the both.

The grassy road is fair and attractive
The woods are no less dark and deep
They take one routinely knowing its end;
No quivering I saw in taking a bumpy one.
Which road had a better claim?

The other is steep and meandering
Covered with leaves, not always straight;
Does it matter if it were black or red?
The heavy foot fall turns it smooth;
Man reaches the Mars and the Moon.

On a square pondering and wondering
A squirrel stays on the big tree nearby.
It screamed at the honking traffic and
The dark smoke belched out from the
Upset stomachs staring at the traffic lights.

The pigeon sighs, the cuckoo sighs
The deer joins them with monkeys,
The rabbits come out of their burrows
The tortoises walk shaking their necks
The tiger laughs. Their chorus asks
Do the roads make a life easy at all?

Thryaksha Ashok Garla
(Chennai, India)

Thryaksha Ashok Garla has been writing since she was a kid. Focusing on the abstract, she likes to ask questions no one has asked and answer questions no one has responded to. Having written over 250 poems, she touches upon themes such as feminism, self-reliance, and love and mostly writes blues. Her work has appeared in several anthologies, and she is currently pursuing psychology. She's an artist and loves to paint.

REBORN

The small lines near her eyes,
Now not the only show of a smile,
As she finally removed the mask,
The grass smelling greener than before.
She looked at the blue skies,
The warm glow in the air around,
She huffed a small laugh,
Lenses did no justice to the real world.
People embracing each other,
Conversation happening in real time,
Not through shrouded screens,
Or half-hearted likes.
The birds' chirping, a rich sound,
Not playing through speakers.
Emotions real and raw again,
Not just for show.
People running to each other,
Not for help but for love.
No more imprisoned thoughts,
The mind ridding its claustrophobia.
Life blossomed again,
In the wake of everything that passed.
Each person stronger than before,
Sharpened like a knife with a stone.
Spilling with everything learned,
Man evolved, still evolving,
Finding our footing once again,
It's over, we can rest now.
A new found self-awareness,
A nod to new reforms,
Each person reborn again,
This is our second chance at life.

A LESSON WELL- LEARNT

My pen tapped no longer,
As I thought of what to write.
My knee bounced no longer,
As I anticipated the light.
I took a deep breath,
With every rattle of my world.
A calm face, and a smile,
As my solution unfurled.
Learnt to work for tomorrow,
And not just for tonight,
My toil replacing crystal balls,
As I determined to do things right.
The pandemic, an ordeal,
But a lesson nonetheless,
Taught me patience and restraint,
All roads to success.

Tuwanda Muhammad
(Atlanta, Georgia, USA)

Tuwanda Muhammad is a poet and playwright based in the United States. Her poetry is inspired by life, scripture, and nature. She has performed at the Tupac Shakur Community Center, Decatur Book Festival, Mother May I? theatre program, Java Speaks, 100 Thousand Poets For Change, and the Wesley Chapel Poetry program. She is the host and producer of It's a Wrap: End of the Year Poetry Reading.

AFTER MIDNIGHT, THE MORNING COMES

My hope is the air in my lungs,
the stride in my step, my spoken name.
Without hope I cannot breathe,
travel or be known.
My life never stands still,
it continues to move with hope

This year hope was my best friend
to keep me going. The hope that
One day, I will be with family again,
One day, I will be with friends again,
One day, I will be with people again,
One day, I will be free again.

Even when my hopes come undone,
when the dreams I dreamt pop like bubbles,
I continue to breathe the fresh air of the morning sun.

What is life without hope? It is a crusty piece
of toast burnt in the oven. A cry that never
sleeps, a resounding echo in a continuous loop.

I need hope. I believe in hope because
after midnight the morning comes;
after midnight the morning comes.

T.W.
(Shangai, China)

Iron dance, a no age. Shanghai writer, senior lecturer/trainer. In the city, to write poetry, organize T·W./technology wisdom writing workshop activities involving poetry, fiction, drama, and love to write literature free talk.

NIGHT'S VEIL

Trees and stones by the lake
have each other' s company
My surprised feet
Stepping on the soft soil
Starting with the way of the heron
Standing by the water
No tweet
Don't sigh for life
The lake has kept all the clouds there
A mysterious cup
I am peaceful
Peace in peace
Liuyun Lake
Someone is coming

Uditi Naagar
(Chennai, India)

Uditi Naagar is a nineteen-year-old from India pursuing her undergraduate degree in Mathematics. She likes writing essays, short stories, and poems on topics that interest her, such as animal welfare, friendship, racism, etc. She won an honorary mention for her short story 'Dreams and Struggles' written for the 'Reflections 2020' conducted by the Konrai foundation, the second place in the essay writing competition organized at 'Exuberance 2020' by St. Francis Institute of Management. She's an athirst reader and enjoys reading different kinds of books.

AFTER THE FALL

The wings now healed
Feet stronger than ever
The sun rose with newfound hope
To a world almost free of fear

Raising its head from its home
Witnessing the beautiful beginning
Of this new life, this new world
Now stronger and smarter

In no time it was ready
To launch off the small nest
Into a world that was oddly different
Yet awfully familiar

Bustling streets and open cafes
Kindness and humanity
Just like it used to be
A world that was different
But just as it used to be.

Vickie Ya-Rong Chang
(Berkeley, California, USA)

The daughter of Chinese immigrants, Vickie Ya-Rong Chang (she/her) was born and raised in the San Francisco Bay Area. In her work as a psychologist and group facilitator, she is dedicated to personal-co lective liberation. A core team member of East Point Peace Academy where she focuses on climate justice and building Beloved Community, she also supports API movement spaces by offering awareness and somatic practices, which are fundamental to her individual and group counseling work. She is strengthened by her connection to the Chinese ancestral lineage including Wudang Mountain; to Sangre de Cristo in New Mexico; and to Arunachula in Tiruvannamalai.

JOY IS HERE

One night moments beyond the dead of winter,
hope will rise and dampen the air

The same tired nightmares will
miraculously transform into
delightful adventures

The stories that haunt you will lay down
with a resigned sigh
in the moonlight of awareness

And you will reach for the longings of the heart
with palms outstretched
a sloppy grin spreading rapidly across
the plains of the face
and the head tilted back with glee

The ancestors dieties and spirits
will dance lilies at your feet
as one life ends
and another begins

THE PRIDE

Inspired by a photo from Chobe National Park in Botswana.
Originally inhabited by the San peoples, also known as Bushmen,
members of the Khoe, Tuu, Kx'a-speaking indigenous hunter-
gatherer groups that span the land known as South Africa.

I turn the thin glossy wisps of wood mutated by man, and I
tumble into an adventure
where a lioness whose face is painted in blood stares at me
boldly across terra water and sky.

Where a pride of lions growl at the crocodiles in the water,
reluctant to cross,
their comfort lying plainly in their closeness,
flank against paw
head against tail
draped playfully on top of one another
once sated from the kill.

Night is time for hunting, each with their singular power and
desire.
One queen hurling forward in the darkness with no hesitation.
Her brother waiting for the cues to launch into the game
of life and death
hunter and hunted.

While I sit in a warm manmade box ten thousand miles
away, living in another world, domesticated like their
unrecognizable cousin, the common cat.

And when night falls and the stars shine from far in the galaxy,
I do not stretch my claws, arch my back, and sink my teeth into
the spine.

381

I do not leap on a Cape buffalo 6x my weight as my sisters and
brothers eagerly join.
My life is not threatened by a cobra that kills my young.

Am I alive?
What hunts me through the long darkness night after night as the cool
globe hiding the rabbit rises and the fiery orb reigns continental plates
away?
What do I hunt in the dead of winter after a year of death
                                                    around me

                                        inside me?

What comes alive in the mysterious pause after sunset before moonrise
with a snarl, conditioned by eons of evolution so without a thought,
I simply act—
the lioness inside alive, powerful, hungry.

What are the giraffes impala zebras elephants hippopotamus wildebeast
warthogs tsessebes that I cry for— especially the massive unpredictable
Cape buffalo that defies reason when the law is survival. Sustaining
fractured ribs, split skulls, red gaping welts, even death from horns and
kicks in the desperate battle.

Oh to be alive on the savanna and wild!
To do what I was born to do, not bred.
To live free as the heart longs.
To race at full speed with no hesitation.

When death comes with my sisters and brothers at
                                        any moment
                                        any night.
To die in the middle of sating my hunger
                                        for life.

Virginia Fernández Collado (Almeria, Ancalucía, España)

Virginia Fernández Collado is a Professor of Business Administration in Secondary Education and holds a Doctorate in Applied Economics besides a Master´s degree in "Fiscal Consulting" from the GADE Business School, Madrid.
She has six books published, her poems have appeared in joint books, and she also coordinated several poetry anthologies.

SUMMER

Selected from the collection
called *Forest*, Fondo Kati, 2020.
Translated by the author.

I live in a wasteland in the world. I walk from me to the center, from the world to the star, from the night to the abyss. I want solitude, shelter, life, singing birds. I am in the desert land, walking towards its center. I choose, from the crack, the wound, from its opening, the sky. Wings flying everywhere, be the apple trees, my house. I believe in trees and mountains, in forests and rivers, in arid expanses and in all the geography through which our laments and our joys travel. I believe in the earth, creator of animals and men. I believe in the sun with which we warm ourselves and thanks to which we contemplate the extreme beauty of the land by which flowers and thorns can live. I believe in the night by which the day becomes beautiful. I believe in the rain that wets us and makes us grow the seed that will feed us. Praise be to the land on which we live and breathe every day. Beloved, what solitude is this that invites recollection? What loneliness do you bring me to? Where will the night stay? Where will the fears go? What loneliness will this be if it is not called snow? Beloved, the rain is trembling like a moon over the sea. He has not seen the stars. He has not seen the fish. The rain has a cloak, everything covers it. He has not seen the sky. Blind, the rain falls. The rain is trembling like a moon over the sea, it is unexpected rain, always unexpected rain. Do not fear the snow, white clouds bring winter. Heaven is a chorus of seraphim. The morning is white, the sea is white, the sky is white. One morning I woke up and white flooded our hearts. But also, the night. The night like a throat that screams, the night like a cliff, the night, the night darkens, the night is my countenance, the night is a forest, the night, an animal that lurks. The rivers die on the maps spilling dry tears. Summer passes.

Wang Fa
(Tangyuan, Heilongjiang, China)

Wang Fa was born on March 21, 1946, in Fuxing Village, Tangyuan County, Heilongjiang Province. His ancestors lived in Gaomi, Shandong. In 1972, he began publishing poems, novels, and film reviews. In 1979, he co-founded the "Eye" private journal with others n Changchun. In 2011, he registered for China Poetry Network and served as editor, host, forum editor, and website deputy editor. He is currently the editor-in-chief of Hong Kong's "the pioneer" poetry magazine, the editor-in-chief of China Changchun's "Sun Pavilion" poetry magazine, ard the editor-in-chief of "Fa Ge's Poetry World". Director of Domestic Channel Department of World Poetry movement. Now lives in Jilin·Changchun.

SPRING

Translated by Bai Shui

This spring is no longer a good time for me
The sound of wind, rain, and endorsement are surging like a tide
Grass, trees, flowers and plague once again covered the world

Poet walking on the ground
Carrying heavy wings
In the dark night, the mind is claustrophobic
Little beast with joy
Sniff out
Bitter grassy fragrance from dark soil

When the dirt is placed on a clean jar
Like a raging fire scorching a river
How to wash children's star-like innocence

I will not use any innocent excuses
Enough to overshadow the cold darkness and injustice

Poet walking on the earth barefoot
Snow horse, thunder, burning cloak
It penetrates the windy season instantly like lightning
The misery of spring
The echo will disappear in the distance

Wang Yagang
(Shangai, China)

Wang Yagang, a native of Shanghai, got his literary works published in magazines and poetry collections. He is currently a Chinese Writers Association member and the Shanghai Pudong New Area Writers Association chairman.

MOON NIGHT AT REED MARSHES
INSCRIPTION FOR LI JINGLIN'S PAINTINGS

Translated by Gui Qingyang

So still, so quiet
So peacefully flowing the moonlight
Around the reed marshes
Shining the waves and ripples light
Enlightenment of the creature in silence
Making life sublimated and purified
Thus reaching the wonderland of the soul
Reed catkins symbolizing the whisk of horsetail
In the hands of True Man
Earlier than frost, earlier than snow
Blown by the wind crossing the sky
Away brushing all noise and all trouble
Of this mortal world
At this very moment the wind is no longer natural
The moon no longer natural
With hibiscus towering above the general

Winston Farrell
(Bridgetown, Barbados)

Winston Farrell presently works as the Cultural Arts Officer at the Barbados Youth Service. An award-winning playwright and recipient of the Frank Colymore Literary Endowment for poetry, Farrell has held Artist/writer in residence at Jefferson Community College and Albany State University in association with the Hudson Valley Writers Group. He graduated from the University of Leeds with a Masters in Theatre and Development Studies. Farrell officiated as the NIFCA Drama/Speech chief judge from 2011-2013 and has also contributed as a Party Monarch chief judge, Sweet Soca, and Pick of the Crop judge over the years. Farrell is well known for his famous Bus Man poem.

CORONA HAIKUS

In 2020
Vision lost in pandemic
Worldly life post-pone

A country locks down
Protocols up petticoats
A country opens

Fresh graves for today
In the factory of the dead
Numbers keep rising

Turning the corner
Like a bandit on the run
Spike waves curve clusters

Thinking about it
Having some friends come over
Just like the old days

Behind the caution
Uncertain of the unknown
Game of wait and see

Mistrust and fake news
As fluid as the flu bug
Flying hand to mouth

Mischief in mankind
Making of a perfect storm
The eyes of science

CORONA the queen

Lies variants and vaccines
A nexus and them
Invariant variants
The never changing changes.

BURNING TRUTHS

There is no fucking phoenix here
in this Rome we call home
No rising out of the ashes
of burnt sugarcane fields

For the ordinary bill and cutlass
Severance paid up in full lies
On a pyre of burning truths
Flames become the only hope

The maid and the butler not exempt
from the firing protocols of the plantation
The modern poor remains essential
and disposable in one breathe.

But as sure as there is a god there is a sankofa
The resurrection of the sufferer flying into a rainbow
Looking back over our trails and trials
Immortal wings flapping forward into futures.

THE LAST MOMENT

There is a shift happening
We can't go back to what we loved and hate
Roses are blooming corps even as we wait it out
It was a long way from us in early march
A few weeks down the line
A grinding halt to spring
How can you just do nothing
Sitting around all day at home
Never enough food parcels in a curfew
We had to send the gifts by mail this year
I remember her name her make up
The mom who could not hug her children
The day she felt like a terrible nurse
The magic of laughter and tears gone
No one should die alone
Will this be the last time we hear the silence
How much longer must we hold on to this emptiness
Before the turn around the corner.

Yudit Shahar
(Petach Tikva, Israel)

Yudit Shahar was born and raised on the outskirts of the Hatikva Neighborhood of Tel Aviv and lives today with her two children in the city of Petach Tkva. "Tikva" ("Hope") is a very significant word in her life story. She studied history at Tel Aviv University and Special Education at the Kibbutz Teachers' Seminary. Since the age of seven, she has been writing poetry. Her poems, primarily of a social and political nature, have been published in journals, anthologies, and newspapers. So far, two poetry bocks have been published and honored with literature prizes.

OPEN IT

Open the window
open it
what do you already have to fear
tear the window
what is already out there
breathe the wild skies
beauty and pain
small fish, rodents, clouds,
life flutters under a knife
drips yearnings
swarms
bus drivers send you a look
sweets-sellers in the *shuk* size you up
you hid life
inside underwear
and covered it in a wide dress,
open it

THE NIGHTINGALE

It was an era of assets-sets-sets
an era of skyscrapers-pers-pers
which spread locusts on the face of the heavens.
It was an era of temples twinkling
where the masses-asses-asses took a knee.

It was the era of the right people-right-right
The era of image-makers
The era of the beautiful-full-full
The era of marketers, designers, spokespersons,
The era of running polls

It was the era of crows crowing
The era of peacocks preening
The magicians made doves
and rabbits-bits-bits disappear.
The liars flowered
necklaces of words-words-words

It was the era of self-decoration
the era of shuddering
the cheats cheated
the pigs pigged out
the poor were tortured
the distressed were stressed-stressed-stressed

and only the nightingale's soul
refused
to stop
singing

About the Editor

Okemwa has published ten poetry collections, including The Gong (Nsemia Inc., 2010), Purgatorius Ignis (Translated to French by Alice-Catherine Carls; Foreword by Sukrita Paul Kumar; Nsemia Inc., 2016), Ominous Clouds (Translated to Norwegian by Gunnar Waerness, to Finnish by Jyrki K. Ihalainen & to Greek by Christos R. Tsiailis; Foreword by Marilena Zackheos; Nsemia Inc., 2018); The Pieta (Translated to Armenian by Hermine Navasardyan; sponsored by Sona Van, 2019); Love from Afro Catalonia (Translated to Catalan by Pau Sabaté; Kistrech Theatre International, 2020), Izabrane Pesme: Selected Poems (Translated to Serbian by Milutin Djurickovic; Alma and Sunčani Breg, Belgrade, 2020); Tisztítótűz/Purgatory (Translated to Hungarian by Balázs F. Attila; AB ART Publisher, Budapest, 2020); and Between the Walls and Empty Spaces (Demer Press, Netherlands, 2021).

Okemwa has also published a short story collection, Chubot, the Cursed One and Other Stories (Nsemia Inc., 2011). He has published three children's books, The Visitor at the Gate, Let us Keep Tiger, and The Village Queen (Paulines Africa, 2009, 2010, 2010). These are in addition to four oral literature texts, Riddles of the Abagusii People of Kenya: Gems of Wisdom from the African Continent (Nsemia Inc., 2011), The Proverbs of the Abagusii of Kenya: Meaning & Application (Nsemia Inc., 2012), Otenyo, a play (Nsemia Inc., 2016) and Oral Poetry of the Abagusii of Kenya (Foreword by John S. Akama; Nsemia Inc., 2020). He has also written five folktales of the Abagusii people of Kenya in the Ekegusii language, namely Ogasusu na Oganchogu (The Hare and the Elephant), Ogasusu na Okanyambu (The Hare and the Chameleon), Ogasusu na Okanyang'au (The Hare and the Hyena), Okang'ombe,

Okanyang'au na Ogakondo (The Cow, the Hyena & the Monkey), and Kerangeti na Kerantina (Kerangeti & Kerantina). Okemwa's novella, Sabina and the Mystery of the Ogre, won the 2015 Canadian Burt Award for African Literature (Kenya). Its sequel, Sabina the Rain Girl (Nsemia Inc., 2019), was selected for the UN SDG 2 Zero Hunger reading list.

Okemwa has co-translated from English to Swahili the works of the following international writers: The Finnish Poet Inger Mari Aikio's The Wind Passes Over Me / Upepo Hupepea Juu Yangu, poems (Nsemia Inc. Publishers, 2018, Ontario/Nairobi); The Hungarian poet Balázs F. Attila's Blue / Zamawati, a poetry collection (Kistrech Theatre International, 2019); Serbian writer Milutin Djurickovic's How the Twins Grew Up, a collection of short stories /Jinsi Mapacha Walivyokua, Mkusanyiko wa hadithi fupi za watoto, (Kistrech Theatre International, 2020); and Hungarian writer István Turczi's Somewhere Budapest/Mahali Fulani Mjini Budapest (Kistrech Theatre international, 2022).

Okemwa is the editor of several international anthologies: The 1112-page poetry anthology, Musings During a Time of Pandemic: A World Anthology of Poems on COVID-19 (2020), 1300-page poetry anthology, I Can't Breathe: A Poetic Anthology of Social Justice (2021), The Griots of Ubuntu: an Anthology of Contemporary Poetry from Africa (2022); and An Anthology of Poems from East Africa and Beyond (2022). He is the editor of the annual Kistrech International Poetry Festival Magazine and co-editor of In the Murk of Life: An Anthology of Poetry, published by Nsemia 2019.

OKemwa's poems have appeared in the Kistrech International Poetry Festival Magazine, Kisii, Kenya; The Noyan Tapan, Armenian weekly newspaper; Mwangaza, The Journal of Literature Students Association University of

Nairobi, Kenya; Echoes Across the Valley, a Kenyan poetry anthology published by EAEP; Art Grakanutyun, Armenian Poetry Anthology; Amaravati Poetic Prism, an International Multilingual Poetry Anthology, India, 2017-2019; The Fund for Cultural Education and Heritage- FEKT; The International Poetry Shelter, Ithaca & Huifeng Poetry Project; Kenya Scholars and Studies Association, KESSA; International Association of Writers-Pjetër Bogdani; and World Poetry Magazine of China.

Okemwa has written forewords and introductions to the following works: John Akama's The Untold Story: Gusii Survival Techniques and Resistance to the Establishment of British Colonial Rule, 2019, Nsemia Inc. Publishers, Nairobi, Kenya; Okoegerera Ekegusii Association's Omogusii: Oboroso, Chinyangi N'emeyega Ya Mwanyagetinge, 2019, Africa Herald Publishing House, Kendu Bay, Kenya; Christopher Okemwa's Musings During a Time of Pandemic: A World's Anthology of Poems on COVID-19, 2020, Kistrech Theatre International, Kisii, Kenya; Christopher Okemwa's I Can't Breathe: A Poetic Anthology of Social Justice, 2021, Kistrech Theatre International, Kenya, Kisii, Kenya; Christopher Okemwa's The Griots of Ubuntu: An Anthology of Contemporary Poetry from Africa, 2022, Kistrech Theatre International, Kisii, Kenya; Anuradha Bhattacharyya's poetry collection Corona Doldrums, 2021, Authorpress, India; Christopher Okemwa's An Anthology of Poems from East Africa and Beyond, 2022, East Africa Educational Publishers, Nairobi, Kenya.

Okemwa participated in a poetry workshop at Poets' House, Northern Ireland, that was run by Janice Fitzpatrick and her late husband James Simmons; participated at the 20th International Poetry Festival in Medellin (Colombia) in 2010, sponsored by Prince Claus Fund; was a guest poet at the 27th Biennale Poetry Festival in Liege (Belgium) in

2012; was a guest-poet at the 3rd Spring and Poetry Festival in Istanbul (Turkey) in 2018; was a visiting poet at the International Poetry Festival of Hanoi (Vietnam) in 2019, and was a creative writing resident at Faber Writers' Residency in Catalonia (Spain) in 2019.

Okemwa earned his Ph.D. degree in performance poetry from Moi University, Kenya. He also holds an MA and a Bachelor of Education degree in literature from the University of Nairobi, Kenya.